THE DARK SIDE OF MODERNITY

JEFFREY C. ALEXANDER

polity

First published in 2013 by Polity Press

Polity Press
65 Bridge Street
Cambridge CB2 1UR, UK

Polity Press
350 Main Street
Malden, MA 02148, USA

ISBN-13: 978-0-7456-4821-7
ISBN-13: 978-0-7456-4822-4(pb)

A catalogue record for this book is available from the British Library.

Typeset in 11 on 13 pt Sabon
by Toppan Best-set Premedia Limited
Printed and bound in Great Britain by the MPG Books Group

For further information on Polity, visit our website: www.politybooks.com

CONTENTS

Suddenly holy Janus in marvelous two-headed form
Thrust his binary face before my eyes.
I panicked and felt my hair spike with fear,
My heart iced over with a sudden chill.

Ovid, *Fasti*

PREFACE AND ACKNOWLEDGMENTS

I first studied social theory at Harvard as an undergraduate during the late 1960s, a time of social and cultural upheaval over modernity. Attending H. Stuart Hughes' lectures on twentieth-century intellectual history, I was taken by his exploration of the irrational in *Consciousness and Society*. When I started writing social theory, the challenge of the irrational and the non-rational continued to haunt me, particularly in the context of the extraordinary difficulties faced by modern, putatively rational societies. The essays assembled here, written over the last 25 years, can be seen as a series of reports on this rumination, which has continued until today. In my struggle to comprehend modernity, Steven Seidman has been a particularly important interlocutor. His critical yet empathic voice has never been distant from the thinking I present in this book, which I dedicate to him.

Each of these essays has been revised, sometimes significantly, and I am grateful, as always, for Nadine Amalfi's editorial assistance in preparing the present versions for publication.

The chapters that follow have been revised in small or large part for publication here. I thank the following publishers for permission to reprint.

Verso Press for "Between Progress and Apocalypse: Social Theory and the Dream of Reason in the Twentieth Century." In J. C. Alexander (1995), *Fin de Siècle Social Theory: Relativism, Reduction, and the Problem of Reason*. (Chapter One).

Allen and Unwin for "The Dialectic of Individuation and Domination: Weber's Rationalization Theory and Beyond." In S. Whimster and S. Lash (eds.) (1987), *Max Weber and Rationality*. (Chapter Two).

Brill for "The Dark Side of Modernity: Tension Relief, Splitting, and Grace." In E. Ben-Rafael and Y. Sternberg (eds.) (2005), *Comparing Modernities: Pluralism Versus Homogenity. Essays in Homage to Shmuel N. Eisenstadt*. (Chapter Three).

Russell Sage Foundation for "Contradictions in the Societal Community: The Promise and Disappointments of Parsons' Concept." In R. Fox, V. Lidz, and H. Bershady (eds.) (2005), *After Parsons: A Theory of Social Action for the Twenty-First Century*. (Chapter Four).

Sage Publications for "Rethinking Strangeness." *Thesis Eleven* 79, November 2004: 87–104. (Chapter Five).

University of California Press for "Towards a Sociology of Evil: Getting beyond Modernist Common Sense about the Alternative to 'the Good'." In M.P. Lara (ed.) (2001), *Rethinking Evil: Contemporary Perspectives*. (Chapter Six).

Lawrence & Wishart Publishers for "Contradictions: The Uncivilizing Pressures of Space, Time, and Function." *Soundings* 16, 2000: 96–112. (Chapter Seven).

Sage Publications for "Social Subjectivity: Therapy as Central Institution." *Thesis Eleven*, 96, 2009: 128–34. (Chapter Eight).

Fudan University Press for "Dangerous Frictions: Conditions of Modernity and Its Possible Repair." *The Fudan Journal of the Humanities and Social Sciences*, 4 (4) (2011): 1–11. (Chapter Nine).

Page vi, from Fasti by Ovid, translated and edited with an introduction, notes and glossary by A. J. Boyle and R. D. Woodward (Penguin Classics, 2000). Copyright © A. J. Boyle and R. D. Woodward, 2000.

INTRODUCTION

To say that modernity has been a disappointment would be understating horrors that continue to endanger the very existence of humankind. Yet to say modernity has been only a nightmare would be telling a one-sided story. Modernity has also been liberating, providing ideals, movements, and institutions that can repair, not only some of its self-inflicted injuries, but cultural and structural disorders that have plagued social life from its beginning.

In Western societies, the once rosy hopes for modernity have faded. The twentieth century produced a series of catastrophes that had been adumbrated in the centuries before. Voltaire, the intellectual hero of the Enlightenment, was deeply anti-Semitic. Thomas Jefferson, the author of the Declaration of Independence, was a slave-holder. Kant, the Enlightenment's most important philosopher, was racist and orientalist. As modernity emerged, so did colonial expansion; as modernity intensified, colonial domination deepened in the name of Enlightenment and civilization. From Napoleon onward, modern nations waged wars for progress with heinous weapons forged by technological reason. In the middle of the twentieth century, Germany, a nation of scientific achievement and Enlightenment *Bildung*, committed genocidal murder against six million Jews and killed millions more innocents and soldiers in a war that almost succeeded in returning Europe to medieval times. Two decades later, the American Air Force tried bombing Vietnam back to the Stone Age. In the years since, social theory

1

and social movements have relentlessly uncovered new forms of irrational prejudice at the very core of Western institutions, from abiding racism and misogyny to orientalism and homophobia (Seidman 2013).

As these shockingly "antimodern" events and qualities have piled up, great social thinkers became critics of modernity itself (see chapter 1, below). Marx had fervently believed that, with the advent of socialism, modernity's basic structures could be saved. After the Holocaust and two world wars, Frankfurt school Marxists came to reject the Enlightenment as such. Speaking the fatalistic language of Weber, Horkheimer and Adorno described the "disenchantment of the world" as "the dissolution of myth and the substitution of knowledge for fancy" (1969). They asserted that Enlightenment reason had become merely instrumental, authentic meanings and responsible feelings impossible, and that culture, having lost its autonomy, was reduced to an industry. Marcuse argued capitalism had so quantified modern mental life that one-dimensional society had entirely suppressed critical thought and moral responsibility (Marcuse 1964).

Suggestions that modernity empties culture of meaning, eliminating the very possibility of morality, have become widespread (Alexander 1995). Such arguments represent an understandable emotional and moral reaction to the traumas of the twentieth century, but empirically they are incorrect. Rather than modernity repressing moral substance and emotional imagination, we must see it as Janus-faced, as blocking and facilitating at the same time. Immensely difficult and deeply destructive, modernity has also produced new technologies of self and society that facilitate far-reaching repairs. A civil sphere has been partially institutionalized, its culture and institutions providing unprecedented opportunities for group incorporation and individual recognition (chapters 6 and 7 below). Ministering to individual rather than collective wounds, psychotherapy has emerged as a central institution in modernity (chapter 8). Modern societies overflow with critical counter-narratives that illuminate political alternatives and frequently demand moral responsibility (Alexander 2006).

One can no longer conceive modernity as representing a sharp break from orders of a "traditional" kind, if, indeed, it were ever possible at all. Decades ago, Umberto Eco already identified a contemporary "return of the Middle Ages," suggesting that a broad spirit of "neo-medievalism" has permeated modern life (1986). We have witnessed the return of the sacred in our time, paroxysms of apocalypse and utopia, romanticism and chivalry, ecstasy and repentance, barbarism and crusades, localism and difference, blood and soil (Holsinger 2007, 2008). There has also unfolded a proliferating attention to signs and icons, the intellectual response to which has been the renewal of semiotic theorizing and hermeneutical methods of interpretation. In contemporary social science, cultural sociology has been one particularly notable disciplinary result of such proliferation.

At the foundation of cultural sociology is the anti-historicist claim that structures of meaning – cultural codes, symbols, and narratives – are a permanent, not transitory element of consciousness and society (Alexander 2003b). As Robert Bellah once put it, "neither religious man nor the structure of man's ultimate religious situation evolves" over historical time; what changes is "religion as a symbol system" (1991). Culture structures remain anchors for collective meanings without which social and individual life is impossible to conceive. Rather than evicting meaning, modernity reformulates cultural structures and subjects them to new strains.

This line of theorizing has been severely constrained by the reluctance of cultural theorists to confront the dark side of modern meaning. For Durkheim and Parsons (chapter 4), simply to sustain culture meant creating social value and moral good; it was the absence of meaning that created instability and evil. Simmel and Eisenstadt seemed to move beyond such an idealizing model of culture, the former identifying the stranger (chapter 5), the latter associating normative institutionalization with tension rather than stability (chapter 3). Neither, however, viewed evil as residing inside the core of modern culture itself. Only Weber tries to theorize both sides of modernity, conceptualizing not only autonomy but also terrifying discipline, the combination of which produce endemic efforts at flight (chapter 2). Yet Weber believed such escape efforts to be doomed: Authentic meanings and emancipatory movement were impossible in the modern age.

3

Ovid imagined Janus first as the ancient god Chaos, presiding over the disorderly mass of matter before the formation of the world, a "crude, unstructured mass, nothing but weight without motion, a general conglomeration of . . . disparate, incompatible elements" inside of which "the sky had no light." Eventually, Ovid tells us, Janus "divided the substance of Chaos and ordered it into its different constituent members," among which was "the strange new figure of Man" (2004). The ancient Romans saw Janus as the god of beginnings and of transitions to the future from the past. With one face, Janus could see backward in time; with the other, he looked forward into the future, marking the midpoint between barbarism and civilization.

Social theorists have struggled to comprehend the Janus faces of modernity. Weber linked this-worldly asceticism to autonomy and domination, yet, while conceptualizing flight, he saw no remedy for rationalization. Simmel pointed to the otherness haunting modernity, yet normalized the stranger. Eisenstadt celebrated ethical transcendence in the Axial Age, but barely acknowledged its capacity for barbarity. Parsons heralded American community, but ignored modernity's fragmentation.

In the chapters that follow, I argue that, inside the culture and structure of modernity, good and evil are tensely intertwined. We should not be naïve about the evils of modernity. Modernity's contradictions cannot be resolved in some magisterial new synthesis. It is a dangerous delusion to think modernity can eliminate evil; new kinds of dangers are produced that challenge new kinds of good. Social theory must accept modernity as Janus-faced. We need to theorize the dangerous frictions of modernity and also lay out new lines for social amelioration and emotional repair. We need to be able to see backward and forward at the same time.

— 1 —

SOCIAL THEORY BETWEEN PROGRESS
AND APOCALYPSE

Social theory is a mental reconstruction of its time, not a reflection but a self-reflection. Art is self-reflection in an iconic and expressive form. Theoretical self-reflection is intellectual and abstract. It leads not to experience and epiphany but to analysis and thought. Social theory cannot induce catharsis, but it can transform understanding. We need social theory if we are going to understand our world. As the great and terrible twentieth century closed and a new one began, this need became even more important.

The thesis of this chapter is that the twentieth century was a unique construction, a historically demarcated world, and that twentieth-century theory is differentiated from earlier theorizing in much the same way. This may be an illusion for future historians to correct. Certainly, neither theory nor history can hope to break out of the self conceptions of their own time. At this point, however, the historical uniqueness of our just completed century seems an empirical fact. It certainly was a social fact, for in this uniqueness most of the participants in that century fervently believed.

To comprehend the underlying motifs of the twentieth century, and eventually its social theory, we must clarify what initially marked the West off from other civilizations, the modern West from earlier periods in its history, and the twentieth century from earlier Western modern societies. This distinguishing notion was "progress" and the possibility of perfection it implied.

All complex societies have had myths about the Golden Age. Only in the West, however, did people seriously begin to think that such a new age might occur in this rather than some other fantastical world. This-worldly conceptions were formulated in Judaism thousands of years ago. If the Jews kept their covenant with God, the Bible promised, God would establish his reign of perfection on earth – what came to be called the millennium. Because Jews were the chosen people, God promised to eventually redeem them. Christianity believed that Christ had been sent to renew this redemptive promise. We have lived in what might be called a millennial civilization ever since.

Yet, Christianity still placed the millennium far off in the distant future. It would certainly not happen in our lifetimes. The lot of human beings on earth, at the present time, could hardly be changed. This religious dualism began to shift with the Reformation, which was much more emphatically this-worldly. Protestants, and especially Calvinists and Puritans, worked hard in this world, with the hope of bringing about the kingdom of God on earth. Such religious belief in the possibility of this-worldly perfection had already received secular sanction in Renaissance humanism, with its earthiness and optimism about improving nature and society. The Enlightenment translated these religious and secular strands of perfectionism into the vocabulary of rational progress. As Becker (1932) suggested in *The Heavenly City of the Eighteenth-Century Philosophers*, Enlightenment thinkers believed in the imminent possibility of a secular golden age.

Perfectionism is the belief that the human world can become the mirror of the divine. This possibility has defined the idealized essence of modernity. To be modern is to believe that the masterful transformation of the world is possible, indeed that it is likely.[1] In the course of modernity, this pledge to worldly transformation has been renewed time and time again. No matter what the disaster, the hope and belief in imminent perfection never disappears. Faith in perfection has informed all the great experiments of the modern world, big and small, good and bad, the incessant reformism and the revolutions launched from the left and from the right.[2]

6

With the Enlightenment and the growth of secular, scientific thought, the ethos of perfectionism became inseparable from the claims of reason.[3] Reason is the self-conscious application of the mind to social and natural phenomena. Through reason, people came to believe, we can master the world. Through this mastery, we can become free and happy. The world can be made a reasonable place. It can be reconstructed. Marx and Hegel produced their own versions of such perfectionism; neither believed in it less fervently than the other.[4]

In the twentieth century this fundamental tenet of modernity was challenged and ultimately changed. The faith in progress was frequently disappointed, and the sense of possibility for perfection diminished. This diminution did not occur in every place and at every moment, of course; in the end, however, it so permeated modern life as to deeply affect its core. Modern became postmodern long before the contemporary period. The experience of the last century came to be seen as a tragic one. The originality of its social theory came from coming to grips with this experience.

The Rational Line: Progress

I do not want to advance this thesis in a polemical or one-sided way. If one does so, the argument becomes myth and caricature, and loses its force. Our understanding of the twentieth century must be more subtle and more complex. To recognize its tragic proportions does not mean to ignore the hopes that it inspired and the real progress it achieved.

From the point of view of the present day, it is possible to look back on that century as a time of wondrous achievement. It is especially possible, and likely, for Americans to do so, but it is not impossible even for Europeans. Doing so reflects the particular historical vantage point of the present day; it also reflects the continuing intensity of the progressivist faith. History can, after all, always be reconstructed in different ways.

If we look back at the beginning of the twentieth century, we can see great hopes. In Germany and in the Austro-Hungarian

Empire, large social democratic parties existed, and their progress appeared to many as inexorable. By pledging themselves to control the market and by demanding full voting rights, these parties promised to incorporate the working classes into industrial economies and to democratize the state.[5]

Similar progressive forces seemed to be expanding in other industrialized nations. In England, radical utilitarians and Fabian socialists had increasing access to social, intellectual, and state power, and Marxian socialism itself was becoming a stronger and more militant force. In environments less hospitable to socialism, liberalism was developing a social program of its own. French "solidarism" and American "progressivism" were viewed as prime examples of the successful mitigation of capitalism's harshest face.

The progressive view of the past century can be sustained by drawing a straight line from these promising developments to the condition of industrial societies today. One can argue that Marxism, liberalism, social democracy, and even democratic conservatism have succeeded in transforming and, indeed, in perfecting modern life.

This rational line can be justified by pointing, for example, to the extraordinary increase in material wealth. Through the rationality of capitalism and industrial production, this affluence has ameliorated the conditions of everyday life throughout most of the class structure of advanced societies. These conditions are not limited, moreover, to consumption in a narrow sense. It is primarily as a result of this material transformation (Hart 1985: 29–49) that deaths in childbirth (for both infants and mothers) have been largely eliminated and that such deadly diseases as tuberculosis have passed from the scene. One may point to the achievements of modern science, both pure and applied, which have contributed to such life-giving disciplines as modern medicine. The series of technological revolutions that have increased material productivity hundreds of times over make Marx's predictions about the exhaustion of capitalism seem not just antique but almost reactionary. We are in the midst of what has been called the fourth industrial revolution, the transformation of information capacity that began with the transistor and miniaturization and, with the computer chip, digitalization, and the world-wide web, has continued on an unprecedented scale.

The rational line can be further sustained by pointing to the expansion of human rights. T.H. Marshall (1964) drew an evolutionary model of the progress from civil to political to social rights. Over the last 40 years, civil and political rights have been extended to religious and racial groups that had been excluded from Western societies for hundreds and sometimes thousands of years. Social rights have been expanded to groups who were considered to be deserving of their unfortunate fates only a century ago – like the physically and mentally disabled. For the first time since the Neolithic revolution ten thousand years ago, women have substantial access to the institutional and cultural centers of society.

These advances may rightly be considered evidence for the advance of reason, and they have been spread to civilizations which did not initially share in the benefits of this-worldly millennial religion. Decolonization extended "European" progress while allowing national aspirations to be freely expressed. Revolution, often the vehicle for decolonization, allowed modernization to spread to less rationalized areas of the world. It, too, can be considered a successful example of the extension of world mastery which has helped perfect life in the modern world.

On these grounds, it may be argued that the twentieth century was a time of progress, that this is not only a plausible view but also a valid one. There are not only many Americans and Europeans arguing this view today, but articulate leaders in India, China, Brazil, and Japan as well. The twentieth century was a good and sensible world. Yes, evil and irrationality still exist, but their origins are outside of us. They stem from traditionalism and antimodernity, with religious fanatics in Arab countries, with tribal hostilities in Africa, with nationalist antagonism in Russia and Israel. Closer to home, they arise in impoverished groups who have not had the access to modernity that education and material comfort provide. When we walk through our modern lives, organizing our lifeworlds with good sense and a modicum of comfort, it seems only reasonable to think that reason has prevailed.

The Dream of Reason

The reality of this social interpretation of the twentieth century is underscored by the fact that it has produced a line of intellectual reasoning, of social theory, that goes along with it. I will call this the dream of reason. It is the image of rationally perfected life in thought, but not of course a reflection of "real," material life alone. Because life is itself filled with ideas, the perfected life is filled also with ideas about perfection. The reasonable life of today can be traced back to the dream of a this-worldly millennium that began thousands of years ago. The millennial dream is religious, the dream of reason post-religious. Still, the dream of reason operates with the metaphysical props of faith exemplified in Hegel two centuries ago.

We can see the dream of reason most distinctly by pointing to four spheres of modern thought: philosophy, psychology, art, and social engineering.

The most characteristic school of twentieth-century philosophy must surely be logical positivism, which believed that any thought worth thinking could be reduced to rational and eventually mathematical propositions. Philosophy from this perspective would be little more than a truth language, a code that would state the conditions for knowing. In this form, philosophy would allow language and thought to transparently reflect the external world. Words are induced from things that actually exist (Wittgenstein 1922). Thought is a rational induction from this reality. Philosophy must hone the relationship between words and things. Metaphysics will be abolished forthwith. Pragmatism framed this philosophical understanding in an American form.

We should not be so blinded by the surreal dimension of modern art that we fail to see that much of aesthetic modernism is consistent with this rationalizing view. There is a clear movement in modernity which argues that art should be sparse, minimal, flat, rational, and "true." It should not be fictive but direct, not personal but objective. The great exemplifications are architecture and prose. At the origin of modern architecture was the aesthetic dictum that form should follow function. Those who created this

10

style (Pevsner 1977) actually believed their buildings represented not fictive design but followed inevitably from the shape of engineering and rational efficiency. While this self-understanding may be false – engineering and efficiency do not have an implicit design – the International Style was of a decidedly rationalist bent, emphasizing straight lines, angles, and flat surfaces (Le Corbusier 1986 [1931]).

A similar demand for directness, simplicity, objectivity and efficiency characterizes twentieth-century prose. According to the model of science, modern prose language should aim to be transparent vis-à-vis its subject matter and denuded of "style" as such, as that notion was exemplified, for example, in Renaissance speech and writing (Lanham 1976). Connotation and ambiguity are pruned from articles and books. In the English language, Hemingway blazed this trail, with his short, flat, journalistic sentences. *Time* magazine made this style the mass language of its day.

In psychology, two contradictory movements reflected this sense of the ultimate reasonableness of the world. According to Piaget's (1972) developmental psychology, adult persons have developed the capacity for universalistic cognition and rule-oriented morality. These capacities emerge from processes inherent in the life process. Individuals become rational because of realistic experiences. Faced with the growing complexity of reality, they act pragmatically and develop new modes of reasoning through trial and error. Behaviorism also saw individuals as acting in straightforwardly rational ways. Pavlov, Watson, and Skinner argued that people are formed not by subjective fantasy but by their environments, that they are molded into whatever they are pushed into being. Like pigeons and well-trained dogs, human beings are rational in a narrow and efficient sense. If we know their past conditioning, we can make predictions about how they will act in the future.

Theories about the possibility of rational planning were reinforced by developmental and behavioristic psychology, but they also constituted an intellectual movement in their own right. Such thought originates in the nineteenth century as a species of secular perfectionism, with people like Saint-Simon, Bentham, and Marx. It became dominant in the twentieth century, elaborated by democratic socialist theorists of the welfare state like Marshall (1964) and Mannheim (1940) and by technocratic communist theorists as well. The belief was that the world can be subjected to rational control, that the whole ball of wax can be molded by reason into a desirable shape. Rawls (1971) is the greatest English-speaking proponent of this faith in perfection through reason. Habermas (1984) elaborated the same faith in a more pragmatic and linguistic idiom.

The Vision of Decline: The Prophecy of Georges Sorel

With few exceptions, these rationalist and optimistic streams of thought, no matter how brilliant and enlightening, did not represent the greatest and most original achievements of twentieth-century social theory. One reason is that they did not represent something really new; they were extensions of the perfectionist thinking of earlier days. But there was another, more important reason. In its rationalist form, twentieth-century social theory could not fulfill its self-reflective task. It could not tell people the essential things they needed to know about the new kind of society in which they lived.

A straight line between the hopes of the turn-of-the-century period and the achievements of the present day cannot be drawn. There is, rather, a tortuous path (Hughes 1966). If the newly dawning century embodied fulsome hopes for a social reform, it was also known as the fin-de-siècle and the "age of anxiety." The dream of reason continued to inspire twentieth-century thought, but it was the nightmare of reason that captured the most profound theoretical imaginations of the age.

As an entrée into this darker side of modernity, we might look briefly at the thought of Georges Sorel, the French revolutionary syndicalist, who published his original and disturbing *Reflections on Violence* in 1908. Earlier I referred to the large socialist workers' parties as carriers for the ideas, forces, and often the reality of progress in that turn-of-the-century period. Sorel conceived of himself as speaking for a very different segment of the community of dispossessed. He insists (1950 [1908]: 66) that there remained

12

large groups of workers, small employers of labor, and farmers – as well as such intellectuals as himself – who bitterly opposed modernity and saw little hope for social progress within its rationalizing frame. These groups provided a constituency for a more extreme left, one cut off from the progressive and ameliorating groups of the socialist center. As Sorel explains, "Parliamentary Socialism does not mingle with the main body of the parties of the extreme left" (ibid. 67).

These unmingling parties were revolutionaries. In one sense, of course, their ideal was not all that dissimilar from the reformers'. They, too, wanted a perfect society ordered by reason. They were certain, however, that such a society could not be institutionalized in the present phase of social life. Reason had become an otherworldly ideal that could be realized only through violent world transformation. Sorel denigrates "the trash of Parliamentary literature." He despises progressives and has no patience for democratic politics. Such appeals to reason, he writes, are "confused"; they serve "to hide the terrible fear" that marks the inevitable tension between social classes. If socialism is to succeed, it must become revolutionary. Rather than appealing to the rationality of the middle and upper classes, socialists must try to make them afraid: "The workers have no money but they have at their disposal a much more efficacious means of action: they can inspire fear." If the bourgeoisie are afraid, Sorel argues, they will become even more repressive. This is all to the good. It unmasks the real, antiprogressive face of society, and will inspire the proletariat to be revolutionary in turn.

Sorel believes that socialism must turn away from social and political reform and toward the program of the general strike. As a collective act of deliberate violence, the general strike will inspire fear and usher in cataclysmic revolution. Associating such violence with the very group that, according to the rational line, embodies reason – the proletariat – Sorel has posed the fateful dichotomy of twentieth-century life. He has opposed violence to reason and equated progress with violence and force. Fifty years later, Sartre (1976 [1968]) would take up violence in much the same way, promulgating it as a means of a liberating debourgeoisification; from Sartre, Fanon (1965) took violence as the model for

13

anticolonial revolt.[6] In important respects, however, Sorel's opposition of violence to reason was more sophisticated; it was certainly more disturbing and more revealing.

Sorel relativized this threat of revolutionary violence by calling
it a myth. Whether there could or, in strategic terms, should be a
violent strike was not Sorel's concern. Violent revolution was a
myth in which workers had to believe in order to maintain their
esprit de corps and to inspire repressive reactions from the ruling
classes. Myth is necessary because people are irrational. They are
moved by impulses, not by "observation of contemporary facts
[or by] a rational interpretation of the present" (ibid: 99). "Infi-
nitely simpler mental processes" are involved. Only by promoting
the myth of violence can socialists reawaken the spirit of alienation and hatred that creates the desire to destroy bourgeois
society.

Sorel's theory was an apologia for left-wing terrorism,[7] and a
prophecy of the irrationality to come.[8] It was also a brilliant and
representative invention of social theory in the twentieth century.
Faced with the disappointment of socialist hopes for progress,
Sorel theorizes that individuals are not as rational as progressive
theory had thought. Moving against the rational line, he establishes a commonality between modern actors and the myth-wor-
shipers of traditional societies. It is not surprising that Sorel himself
wavered between revolutionary left and right. He abandoned
rationality not just as an explanation of human action but as a
normative stance. He advocates irrationality in its more violent
form. This is where Sorel's thought differs from the more important twentieth-century social theory we examine below. For while
Sorel understood the pathologies of modernity, he could think of
no way to overcome them.

The Degenerate Line: Irrationality

Before we get to this theory, we need to examine the social life
upon which it reflected. It can be argued that in twentieth-century
life there was a real declension, a decline that for many made
progress seem like a dream, or even a myth.

14

Since we have been thinking about Sorel, let us begin with socialism. Marxists and utopians alike had considered socialism (via revolution or reform) to be the very embodiment of reason. For Marx, communalization would overcome the alienation of reason and the subjectivity upon which capitalism was based. As the twentieth century unfolded, however, it became increasingly clear that revolutionary movements of the left often intensified the alienation of reason in drastic ways.[9] This counter-intuitive fact should not be understood in essentialist terms. It has nothing to do with some inherent perversity of revolutionary action but with the sociological conditions under which revolutions typically emerge. Revolutionaries represent groups who have been subject to severe oppression and strains. Typically, they have been excluded from the legitimate centers of their societies and often from their very societies themselves; they have been denied access to education, subjected to despicable prejudices, impoverished, often jailed, sometimes tortured and murdered.

None of this mitigates what Marx himself would surely have regarded as the savage degradation of the revolutionary tradition in the twentieth century. In their alienation, revolutionaries, in and out of power, not only advocated distorted and caricatured thought and speech but often acted barbarously, engaging in systematic force and fraud. For several decades after the outbreak of the Russian Revolution, not only socialists but also a wide range of thoughtful people regarded communism as a legitimate carrier of reason. The true nature of Soviet communism was masked by its claims to reason and scientific accuracy. Wealth, technology, literacy, high culture, hygiene, and class inclusion were the perfectionist references for official communist rhetoric.

It eventually became clear to many that this revolutionary society made of the hopes for perfection a bitter joke. Lenin initiated, and Stalin established (Johnson 1983: 49–103), a system that suppressed the very exercise of reason. Mao, Ho Chi Minh, Kim Jong-il, and Eastern European puppet rulers followed in their wake. Twentieth-century communism was more like the medieval church than a model for rationality and progress (Aron 1957). Ruled by an ideological pope and directed by a clerisy of party faithful, official communism spread the dogma of the proletarian messiah, whose message was interpreted pragmatically in histori-cally appropriate ways. Reason was monopolized by this com-munist church; it was impossible for private individuals to possess it. For the masses, violence was the only recourse. Soviet com-munism subjected first counterrevolutionaries, then conservatives, kulaks, Jews, Christians, and "other" nationalities, and eventually their own cadre, to unprecedented repression. Once in power, communist parties – these purported vanguards of reason and progress – institutionalized vocabularies of double-think and systems of thought control that came to symbolize the nightmares of reason in our time.[10]

Murder and massive political repression in Mao's China; geno-cidal barbarity in revolutionary Cambodia and dreary failure in its occupiers, Vietnam; the overwhelming inadequacies of centrally planned state economies: For intellectuals hoping for human prog-ress, what was left of the revolutionary dream of reason? The communist version of this dream became exhausted two centuries after it began. Intellectual disillusionment with the progressive promise of socialism and communism became one of the most distinctive developments of the late twentieth century (Alexander 1988a).[11]

I have not begun with communism because it is the unique embodiment of bad faith and irrationality. This is the line of the conservative right, and a cop-out intellectually and morally. One must acknowledge that antiprogress and antireason occurred throughout Western societies, in capitalist and democratic coun-tries as well.

The rational line describes the twentieth century as involving gradual democratization, the extension of rights and privileges to the lower classes, the opening up of ghettos, and the persistent spreading of secular rationality throughout society. But, even before the twentieth century got under way, much darker forces were beginning to brew. By the 1880s one could observe on the continent, in France and in Southern and Central Europe, a growing reaction against progressive forces. In the middle and upper classes powerful advocates of dictatorship and violence emerged. In Germany, a mystical and backward-looking *Volk* ideology fermented (Mosse 1964), spreading throughout the

16

intellectual classes (Ringer 1969). In France, there was a sickening turn toward nationalist anti-Semitism. In the United States, the rigidly segregationist policies of Jim Crow spread through the Southern states, and nativism – cultural prejudice and social mobilization against foreign-born immigrants and citizens – became an imperious collective psychology in the North.

These irrationalist forces fed directly into the First World War, the cataclysm that separated what afterward looked like an age of innocence from the wasteland that followed (Fussell 1975).[12] Sometime between 1919 and 1921, when he was the British Secretary of State, Winston Churchill jotted down on a piece of War Office stationery a retrospective whose embittered and apocalyptic tones captured the profound disturbance this war gave to the vision of progress.

> All the horrors of all the ages were brought together, and not even armies but whole populations were thrust in the midst of them . . . Every outrage against humanity or international law was repaid by reprisals . . . No truce or parley mitigated the strife of the armies. The wounded died between the lines: The dead mouldered into the soil. Merchant ships and neutral ships and hospital ships were sunk on the seas and all on board left to their fate, or killed as they swam. Every effort was made to starve whole nations into submission without regard to age or sex. Cities and monuments were smashed by artillery. Bombs from the air were cast down indiscriminately. Poison gas in many forms stifled or seared the soldiers. Liquid fire was projected upon their bodies . . . When all was over, Torture and Cannibalism were the only two expedients that the civilized, scientific, Christian States had been able to deny themselves: and they were of doubtful utility. (Quoted in Johnson 1983: 14–15)

During the decades following the war's end, such activities would no longer arouse astonished indignation. They became everyday occurrences of the twentieth century.

In the chaos and devastation that followed in the wake of the First World War, there emerged at the end of the first third of the century what to rational progressives seemed an historical impossibility: the outbreak in Europe not of revolutions of the left but of counterrevolutions of the right. In Germany, Austria, Italy, and Spain, radical right-wing movements came to power and began to dismantle the rational and progressive apparatuses of their

17

respective societies. This reactionary movement reached its zenith in Germany, and the results are well known. Rather than the promotion of civility and inclusion, there was the genocidal murder of large segments of the carriers of progress, not only Jews but also intellectuals, communists, socialists, scientists, free-thinkers, homosexuals, gypsies, Slavs, and Christian idealists alike.

Alongside the spread of rational understanding, there emerged in the course of the twentieth century brutality and violence on an unprecedented scale. The century invented total war, war to the death, war against not only professional armies but the masses of civilian populations. Americans tend to be less sensitive to these dark developments because none of that century's wars were fought on its continental soil. It is a critically significant fact, however, that liberal democratic countries became full participants in the ideology and practice of total war (Gibson 1986; Johnson 1983). Faced with Hitler's attack on Britain in the summer of 1940, Churchill wrote that "when I look around to see how we can win the war I see that there is only one sure path . . . and that is an absolutely devastating, exterminating attack by very heavy bombers from this country upon the Nazi homeland" (quoted in Rhodes 1988: 469). The leader who once had been repelled by total war had now come to embrace it. Even before dropping atomic bombs on Japan, allied bombing killed 260,000 Japanese and injured more than 400,000 more (Johnson 1983: 423). In their battle against the ruthless National Liberation Front in the first Indo-Chinese war, the French engaged in systematic terror and torture. In their own Indo-Chinese war, the Americans waged blanket bombing, with the intention, in President Johnson's words, of "bombing Vietnam back to the stone age." In contemporary America, one of history's most democratic nations, the massively funded Central Intelligence Agency (CIA) organized secret classes on torture techniques for the military cadres of dictatorial nations; afterward, it gave them the facilities to carry them out. In the early years of the century after, the CIA practiced torture itself.

In part because of continuous warfare, the twentieth century sponsored the spread of charismatic executive authority on an unprecedented scale. In Germany, China, the Soviet Union, Argentina, and Italy, leaders became living icons for their sometimes

18

adoring, sometimes terrified, but often mesmerized and surprisingly compliant populations. In democratic countries, charismatic executive authority never disappeared. In the twentieth century, the cult of the personality became increasingly essential for national integration and effective government (Harden 1974).

Even when the darkest shadows of antimodernity were avoided, the twentieth century was haunted by a sense of disappointment with modern life. In relatively successful countries, boredom and ennui often overshadowed a sense of individual and collective purpose (Keniston 1964). One of the most revealing phenomena of our time has, indeed, been the continuing attempt by those who have managed to avoid the most awful modern brutality to escape from the very progressive forces, ideas, and institutions that have allowed them to be spared. People flee from the demands of this-worldly perfection to the romantic alternatives of various addictions – to drugs and alcohol, to escapist religions, to visions of nirvana of a mystical and other-worldly kind (see chapter 2, below).

The Nightmare of Reason

The historical declension of twentieth-century life had a pronounced effect on its intellectual thought. Reason was experienced as a hollow shell; progress as inconceivable, often as undesirable. The very possibility of a higher point, an "end" toward which society should strive, was thrown into doubt.

When social theory is caught up in the dream of reason, it is post-religious but relies on a metaphysical prop. When it articulates the nightmare of reason, it is post-religious without metaphysics. Paul Tillich, a major twentieth-century theologian who lived without the dream, described modern individuals as adrift and alone, without the traditional support of God. Yet, Tillich (1952) maintained that this condition demanded greater strength and even greater faith, drawing from Sartre the notion that the modern situation demands "the courage to be." Nietzsche drew the opposite conclusion, one more characteristic of the dark line itself. God is dead, reason is a lie, and abstract reasoning lifeless

19

and corrupt. We must escape from our present condition by transcending it. One way to do so is by submerging individual selves and identifying with a supra-moral superman.

But let us turn from this prophecy of alternative societies to efforts at creating alternative worlds of thought. Earlier, I identified four intellectual currents of embodied reason. Here I outline anti-rationalist postures that developed as alternatives. These alternative orientations crystallize the sharp departures from rationality and progress that characterize twentieth-century time.

Twentieth-century philosophy began with logical positivism and the confidence that analytic thought could know the truth. It ended with hermeneutics, a philosophy which maintains that knowing reality in a manner that separates it from subjectivity is epistemologically impossible. Logical positivism was bold, ambitious, predictive. Hermeneutics is modest, exploratory, tentative, regarding the mere description of the object as a herculean task. In earlier (1922) Wittgensteinean philosophy, words can reflect things; they are based in reality. In Wittgenstein's later philosophy – *Philosophical Investigations* (1968 [1945]) – words refer not to reality but to themselves. We do not touch reality; we think within a self-referential cocoon of other thoughts and words. Saussure (1959 [1911]), the founder of structural linguistics and semiotics, made much the same point. There is no way to go from objects, from reality, to the word-thoughts that characterize them. Between words and objects there is only an arbitrary relation. Influenced by logical positivism, earlier philosophy of science was concerned with the conditions for truth, verification, and the evolutionary progress of knowledge. Much of postpositivist philosophy of science glories in irrationality, asserts incommensurability, and theorizes apocalyptic revolutions (Kuhn 1962; Rorty 1979; for critique, see Alexander 1992c and Reed 2011).

Earlier I discussed contemporary aesthetics in terms of minimalism, realism, directness, and linearity. Much more widely recognized is the aesthetic movement in the opposite direction, toward surrealism and antirealism. Particularly in the visual arts and in avant-garde literature, there has been the destruction of the notion of a transparent reality. Artists neither refer to nor rely upon the rationality of human beings. Over the *longue durée*, the

20

discontinuities are striking: from Ingres to Abstract Impressionism by way of Cubism; from Beethoven to Webern by way of Strindberg; from George Eliot and Tolstoy to Beckett and Pynchon by way of James and Woolf. Interpretation theory reflects a similar trajectory. Earlier critics examined authors' intentions, historical contexts, and thematic development within actual texts. Beginning with New Criticism, these standards and practices became less applicable. The complexity and irrationality of motive made authorial intention impossible to discover. Similar difficulties accrue to the study of historical context. With Derrida, lack of confidence in rationality increased to the point that one cannot be certain there is a text.

Freud created the psychological alternative to the rational optimism of developmental and behavioral approaches. Since assumptions about motives are the bedrock of social theory, such depth psychology had a particularly powerful impact, whether orthodox, Jungian, or humanistic. Instead of rational motive, psychoanalysis begins with the passionate, moralistic, and irrational actor. In contrast to the self-confident and reactive individual, the self is viewed as fragmented, contradictory, and difficult to find. Against the notion that reality is either obviously visible or increasingly becoming so, depth psychology emphasizes the difficulty of reality-testing and the omnipresence of distortion. Rather than an innate quality, rationality is something that may take years of treatment for an actor to learn (see chapter 9, below).

The intellectual alternatives to social engineering are at first sight less obvious. Theorists do not argue that society is impossible to change. They do, however, suggest that the standards for promoting and valuating change are neither rational nor capable of providing accurate evaluations. Oakeshott (1962) developed this approach in its conservative form, arguing that social change is encrusted by custom and inherently incremental, and that efforts to plan change rationally only blind actors to such facts. Walzer (1983) and other "internalist" critics of Rawls and Habermas developed this alternative more critically. They argued that justice cannot be understood in terms of abstract criteria and transcendental principles. It must be theorized from within the cultural terms of particular spheres of life. Social movements that ignore these structures encourage the domination and violence that has characterized the degenerate line of twentieth-century life.

Social Theory as a Bridge between Two Worlds

Many of the great thinkers who initiated twentieth-century social thought participated in two worlds. They experienced both the dream of reason and the nightmare that followed in its wake. They came to early maturity as believers in science, evolution, and progress. One thinks here of Freud's first career in psycho-physiology, Weber's pre-breakdown quasi-Darwinian writings in political economy and comparative history, Durkheim's early scientism, Wittgenstein's logical positivism. At a certain point, however, these thinkers came face to face with the darkness and irrationality of their times. When Weber wrote, just after the turn of the new century, that "the rosy blush of . . . the Enlightenment [is] irretrievably fading" (1958 [1904–5]: 182), he gave expression to the darker perception that characterized an entire generation.

For many of these thinkers, the First World War symbolized their disillusionment. In his lecture to German students in the immediate wake of war, Weber rejected out of hand the evolutionary hope for reason:

> I may leave aside altogether the naïve optimism in which science – that is, the technique of mastering life which rests upon science – has been celebrated as the way to happiness. Who believes in this? – aside from a few big children in university chairs or editorial offices. (1946c [1917]: 143)

Three years before that war began, Durkheim wrote that "we are going through a stage of transition and moral mediocrity."

> The great things of the past which filled our fathers with enthusiasm do not excite the same ardor in us . . . The old gods are growing old or already dead, and others are not yet born. (1965 [1911]: 475)

Just after the war began, Freud conceived it as representing the disillusionment thinking people felt with the rationalist promises of the past.

22

We are constrained to believe that never has any event been destructive of so much that is valuable in the common wealth of humanity, nor so misleading to many of the clearest intelligences, nor so debasing to the highest that we know. Science herself has lost her passionless impartiality; in their deep embitterment her servants seek for weapons from her . . .

When I speak of disillusionment, everyone at once knows what I mean . . . We were prepared to find that wars between the primitive and the civilized peoples [and] wars with and among the undeveloped nationalities of Europe or those whose culture has perished would occupy mankind for some time to come. We had expected the great ruling powers . . . who were known to have cultivated world-wide interests, to whose creative powers were due our technical advances in the direction of dominating nature, as well as the artistic and scientific acquisitions of the mind – peoples such as these we had expected to succeed in discovering another way of settling misunderstandings and conflicts of interests. (1963 [1915]: 107–8)

Just as Wittgenstein had been "a happy sunny child" in Vienna, so "his English acquaintances from before 1914 knew him as capable of great gaiety" (Janik and Toulmin 1973: 177). During the war, Wittgenstein fought for Austria on the front lines.

From 1919 on, he became a lonely and introverted figure. He admitted to having been impressed by Oswald Spengler's *Decline of the West*, and he retreated more and more into ethical attitudes of extreme individualism and austerity. (ibid.)

After the war's end, even as the *Tractatus* made him famous, Wittgenstein disappeared from the intellectual world. He taught school in a small peasant village and later became a gardener. When he returned to Cambridge and academic life in 1929, he did so with an outlook deeply at odds with his early, logical positivist phase. He had given up on progress in the conventional sense. "When we think of the world's future," he wrote in 1929 (1980: 3e), "we always mean the destination it will reach if it keeps going in the direction we can see it going in now; it does not occur to us that its path is not a straight line but a curve, constantly changing direction." These curving changes, Wittgenstein was certain, would bring ruin: "The earlier culture will become a heap of rubble and finally a heap of ashes" (ibid.).

23

Cleansed of their earlier innocence, these thinkers devoted themselves to explaining how this darkness could have come about. Yet, if they abandoned the dream of reason, they did not reject rationality as a normative goal. To explain irrationality constituted the principal intellectual challenge of their lives. They would do so in order to preserve the values of modernity in a less naïve, more mature form.

Freud spent his later life outlining the pathways of unconscious irrationality. While allowing that the result of psychoanalysis would not be utopia but simply common unhappiness, he insisted that this was far preferable to the fantasies of psychosis. Psychoanalysis could not eliminate the influence of the unconscious, but it could reduce its ability to distort reality. "Where id was," Freud suggested hopefully, "there ego shall be."

Weber demonstrated how modern rationality had historically arisen from religious commitments, and he believed that "world flight" would be the most common reaction of modern people once these commitments were withdrawn. He condemned these flights and any attempt to restore the metaphysical world. The secular rationality that was the heir to religious rationalization, he insisted, represented the only possible hope for humankind.

In his later work, Durkheim described how the mythical and symbolic underpinnings of modern thought made any conception of narrowly rational behavior obsolete. At the same time, he hoped that his exposure of the social foundation of religion would allow the symbolic dimension to be expressed in a non-deistic form, freeing individual and social cognition to be disciplined by the scientific method.

The case for a continuing commitment to reason is more complex with Wittgenstein. Alone among this first generation of great twentieth-century theorists, he experienced a second world war. Is it surprising that in 1947, after this second shattering experience, he would ask whether it is so "absurd . . . to believe that the age of science and technology is the beginning of the end for humanity," or that he would entertain what he called a "truly apocalyptic view of the world" in which "the idea of great progress is a delusion" (1980: 56e)? When he introduces his *Philosophical Investigations*, that late great poetic reconstruction of ordinary language, Wittgenstein does so in a markedly subdued and pessimistic way:

> I make them public with doubtful feelings. It is not impossible that it should fall to the lot of this work, in its poverty and in the darkness of this time, to bring light into one brain or another – but, of course, it is not likely. (1968: vi)

This late theory of the conventionalized nature of ordinary language explained the impossibility of denatured objectivity in an extraordinarily lucid and rational way. Even while he expressed skepticism about "the idea that truth will ultimately be known" (1980 [1947]: 56e), Wittgenstein continued to see "clarity [and] perspicuity as valuable in themselves" (1980 [1930]: 7e).

The most significant social theorists of the middle and latter twentieth century matured within the framework created, not by the progressive rationalism of earlier modernity, but by Freud, Durkheim, Weber, Wittgenstein, and other thinkers of a similarly "post" modern cast. Keynes was weaned on the anti-utilitarian Platonism of Moore, and he developed a radically new theory of the irrationality of capitalist investment that could only have been drawn from Freud. Lévi-Strauss grew up on Durkheimian anthropology and structural linguistics. Sartre cut his intellectual eye-teeth on Husserl. Marcuse matured with Heidegger, Freud, and Lukács. Parson's intellectual forebearers were Weber, Pareto, and Durkheim.

These more contemporary thinkers differed from their illustrious predecessors only in the fact that they never experienced an epistemological break; their commitment to postmodern thought was nourished by a similar confrontation with the darkness of modern life. Keynes rejected his earlier aestheticism after he was horrified by the barbarism of the Great War and politicized by the nationalistic stupidity of the peace treaty that followed. In the middle of the 1930s, Lévi-Strauss fled to the Brazilian jungle and immersed himself in savage thought because of the repulsion he felt for the mechanization of modern society and the cold, abstract reasoning it employed.[13] Sartre lived at such a distance from French society that he experienced the Second World War almost as a relief (Hayman 1987: 149–78). He wrote *Being and*

Nothingness in a German prisoner-of-war camp, and he took humanity's confinement in "non-being" as characterizing modern society as such. The true condition of being, Sartre wrote, is anguish; to talk about ideal values is only bad faith. Even if he turned in his later work to evolutionary progressivism, Parsons conceived of his great first book as a response to the double shadow of fascism and Stalinism: "Various kinds of individualism have been under increasingly heavy fire [and] the role of reason, and the status of scientific knowledge ... have been attacked again and again" (1937: 5). Marcuse was so traumatized by the twentieth century that he regarded even democratic industrial societies as totalitarian. "The fact that the vast majority of the population accepts, and is made to accept, this society," he wrote (1964: xiii), "does not render it less irrational and less reprehensible."

Yet, even as these later twentieth-century thinkers were haunted by the nightmare of reason, they also refused to accept cataclysmic destruction as humankind's necessary fate. Keynes devoted himself to creating a theory that revived hope for human economy in a post-perfectionist form. Lévi-Strauss, despite his fatalistic ruminations, regarded his life's work as a scientific contribution and urged other rational thinkers to resist the temptations of historicist thought. Sartre insisted that human beings do have the capacity for freedom, and he strenuously argued, in his fiction as well as in his philosophy, for this responsibility to be taken up.[14] Parsons tried to demonstrate, in his early voluntaristic theory, that the internalization of values would provide the basis for a more mediated and secure freedom. Marcuse insisted that transcendence was possible, if only his contemporaries would return to their innately human capacity for critical thought.

Conclusion

H. Stuart Hughes (1966) entitled his examination of French social thought in the interwar years *The Obstructed Path*. His thesis was that French society, and French social theory, had strayed off

26

the normal, expected pathway of rationality and democracy into mysticism, radicalism, alienation, and antimodernity. My argument in this chapter questions such an "exceptionalist" view of antimodernity. Twentieth-century history has been tortuous, and the line of modern social theory reflecting on this development has been obstructed. It is not just French theory between the wars that reflected alienation, radicalism, and irrationalism, but the most original thrusts of twentieth-century theory itself.

It is American thought in the twentieth century that has been exceptional, precisely because it has remained relatively untortured and perfectionist, confident in the unobstructed access to rationality of modern life. For the postwar period, Parsons and Rawls provide the sociological and philosophical illustrations of this rationalist optimism, and Hughes' first important book represents this bias in the discipline of history. *Consciousness and Society* (1958) brought the Whiggish thesis of *The Structure of Social Action* (Parsons 1937) into the domain of intellectual history. Hughes viewed the recognition of the irrational in European thought and the surreal in its art as a deepening of progressive self-reflection; the bitter, tragic, and enormously destabilizing social and intellectual origins of this turn away from rationality go unrecognized.

A taut dialog between pessimism and optimism, reason and unreason, defined social theory in the twentieth century. Suspended between perfection and apocalypse, what marks off the greatest of that century's theorists was their attempt to mediate these dichotomies. While they abandoned positivism and no longer saw their times as embodying the dream of reason, most did not give up on science as hope or reason as possibility. They recognized the omnipresence of irrationality with regret. Their theories are devoted to showing how the irrational works, in different spheres, in different modes, with different results. They conduct these demonstrations by exercising their reason, and they use their hard-won understandings to outline a pathway to a better life. This life would recognize the ineradicable place of irrational experience and the continuing need for meaning. By so augmenting "modernist" understanding, it would be possible to create forms of social life that meet human needs in a less restrictive way.

While this form of life has not yet emerged, as the third millennium of Western history begins it remains a possibility devoutly to be wished. Only by comprehending the transformation of twentieth-century intellectual life will contemporary social theory be able to contribute to this task.

AUTONOMY AND DOMINATION: WEBER'S CAGE

Social theory is committed to empirical standards of truth. It is tied, as well, to the metaphysical demand for reflective equilibrium (Rawls 1971). While, more than any other modern theorist, Max Weber insisted that scientific social theory be absolved of metaphysical ambition, he was also obsessed with the meaning of modern life. This paradox was far from accidental. We will see that it reflected Weber's understanding of the fate of meaning in a secular world. I will argue, indeed, that Weber's empirical sociology establishes the fundamental boundary conditions for rational reflection about the fate and possibilities of the modern age.

Like other great theorists of his time, Weber began his intellectual life with beliefs firmly rooted in the nineteenth century. Though more bellicose in his nationalism than some, he shared the general intellectual faith in the progress that lay open for Western societies. He felt that the rational transformation of nature and the rational organization of society were positive developments well within human reach, and he linked these political and economic changes to increasing the freedom of modernity.

In 1897 Weber suffered a nervous breakdown. When he emerged from this period of emotional and intellectual mortification, he was not only a different person but a chastened thinker. He was prepared, in a way he had not been before, to reflect on the dark side of modernity. While this new perspective is clearly evident

29

from the appearance of *The Protestant Ethic and the Spirit of Capitalism* in 1904, like many others in his generation Weber expressed such sentiments most pointedly in his reactions to the First World War, an event that seemed to sum up the prospects of the new age. "Not summer's bloom lies ahead of us," he told German students in his now famous lecture on politics as a vocation, "but rather a polar night of icy darkness and hardness" (Weber 1946a [1917]: 128).

Weber explicitly linked such despair about the future course of the twentieth century to his disillusionment with the social theory of the nineteenth. In his companion lecture on science as a vocation, he scorned "the naïve optimism" according to which science "has been celebrated as the way to happiness." To interpret in this way what is, after all, a mere "technique of mastering life" is a sign of immaturity. "Who believes in this," he asked students rhetorically, "aside from a few big children in university chairs or editorial offices?" (Weber 1946c [1917]: 143).

Weber is suggesting that a mature thinker must sever the link between cognitive explanation and existential salvation, a connection he traces back to the time when religion still dominated human thought. He had discovered an effort to establish just this kind of relationship in his work on Puritanism. Asking his students to recall Swammerdam's exaltation – "Here I bring you the proof of God's providence in the anatomy of a louse" – Weber suggests they see in this statement "what the scientific worker, influenced (indirectly) by Protestantism and Puritanism, conceived to be his task: to show the path to God" (Weber 1946c [1917]: 142). For a contemporary person, however, maintaining this linkage would be regressive and intellectually immature; it fails to come to terms with what, in Weber's view, is the necessarily naturalistic character of explanation in the secular age.

"An empirical explanation has to eliminate as causal factors," Weber insisted, all "supernatural interventions" (Weber 1946c [1917]: 147). To accept a supernatural cause is to accept the teleological notion that natural events have occurred for some higher purpose, that their cause is neither efficient nor mechanical but derives from an ethical ambition. Since modern science was first promoted by religious men, it is not surprising that in the beginning even naturalistic explanations were squeezed into this teleological frame. But once the full implications of science are understood, its effect must inevitably be exactly the opposite. "If these natural sciences lead to anything," Weber suggests, "they are apt to make the belief that there is such a thing as the 'meaning' of the universe die out at its very roots" (Weber 1946c [1917]: 142). Not to understand this reveals a disturbing lack of inner strength. "Who – aside from certain big children who are indeed found in the natural sciences – still believes that the findings of astronomy, biology, physics, or chemistry could teach us anything about the *meaning* of the world?" (emphasis in original).

Science, then, has contributed to the icy darkness that lies ahead. A world where the very hope for over-arching meaning has died out at its roots is not a happy or reassuring prospect. Yet Weber clearly wants to suggest another, quite different implication of science as well. By separating causal explanation and existential evaluation, science offers the potential for individual autonomy. Science offers a mundane technique of calculation available to every person. The goal of scientific training is "to present scientific problems in such a manner that an untutored but receptive mind can understand them and – *what for us is alone decisive* – can come to think about them independently" (Weber 1946c [1917]: 134, emphasis added). This second implication must not be denied if Weber's sociology is to be properly understood.[1]

Weber's sociology is defined, and at the same time also limited, by the dilemma he has just described. On the one hand, there is disillusionment and existential despair that psychological maturity and cultural integrity cannot be sustained. On the other, there is real evidence for the increasing autonomy and strength of the individual. These poles embody the paradox of the twentieth century. After he recovered from his nervous breakdown, Weber devoted the rest of his life to understanding how both could be true.

How have we come to a condition of "icy darkness and hardness," which threatens to extinguish human life yet at the same time provides the only resources for making human freedom finally possible? It was to answer this question that Weber suggested his master concept of rationalization. Rationalization is at once enervating disenchantment and enlightening empowerment. It has led to increased freedom and at the same time facilitated internal and external domination on an unprecedented scale. The ambiguity is intended. Rationalization is at once a terrible condition, the worst evil, and the only human path for liberation.

Rationalization as Individuation

Those who have emphasized the critical thrust of Weber's rationalization concept (e.g., Mitzman 1970) have, not surprisingly, failed to appreciate that it also implies the increasing freedom of individuals from the tyranny of forced belief.[2] "Increasing intellectualization and rationalization," Weber acknowledges, does not mean that there has actually been increased knowledge about the "conditions under which one lives." This would limit rationalization to a cognitive force. Weber wants to get at something else, and something more – to the individual autonomy that makes such increased cognitive knowledge possible.

> It means something else, namely, the knowledge or belief that if one but wished one *could* learn it at any time. Hence, it means that principally there are no mysterious incalculable forces that come into play, but rather that one can, in principle, master all things by calculation. This means that the world is disenchanted. One need no longer have recourse to magical means in order to master or implore the spirits, as did the savage, for whom such mysterious powers existed. Technical means and calculations perform the service. This above all is what intellectualization means (Weber 1946c [1917]: 139, emphasis in original).

World-mastery, or at least the potential for it, has emerged because of rationalization. Humans have replaced God as the masters of their destiny. Modern people are governed, or at least would like to think of themselves as being governed, by institutions that are human-made, that have been constructed for their effectiveness in achieving human goals. In principle, leaders are held accountable for the way these institutions work.

If this sounds suspiciously like the nineteenth-century outlook that Weber designed his theory to replace, this is because a crucial qualification has been left out; in no sense did Weber conceive this rationality to be natural or inherent. The point of his life's work is to show that the very opposite is the case. Intellectualization, he believed, rested upon the most unnatural motivation, led to the most abstracted orientation, and inspired the most desiccated organization that the world had ever known. Far from rationality being inherent, it must be understood as the result of a long and complicated evolution of irrational, religious belief. The anti-religious nature of the modern world has a religious base. This appears to mark an inconsistency, but it would be considered so only for nineteenth-century thought. Weber holds that only if the irrational basis of rationality is accepted can the tortuous development of rationality properly be understood and the precarious condition of individual autonomy be appreciated.

To understand what modern rationalization entails, what it allows and what it proscribes, one must understand from what it has emerged. The religious world we have lost addressed the meaning of life in a particular way; it harnessed all the different elements of life to the ethical goal incarnated in the godhead. This single goal sat atop a cultural hierarchy. It was the *telos* towards which every other dimension of culture oriented. Artistic expression, understanding of the truth, love between human beings, material success, political power – all were to be conceived as serving this ethical end, as expressions of this ultimate goal.

Weber usually turned to Tolstoy as the modern who best articulated this anti-rationalistic spirit, for the Russian's later work displayed the kind of radical spiritualization that Weber was trying to describe. Tolstoy is not content to let events "simply happen" in a mechanistic way; he is bent on avoiding the naturalistic conclusions to which his literary realism would seem logically to lead. The humiliation of Anna Karenina and the death of Ivan Ilych are both turned into events that "reveal" a higher meaning. Tolstoy places each event in a teleological framework, suggesting that it was fated for each to turn out as it did.

Though Weber is sympathetic with Tolstoy's spiritual yearning, he rejects it as a principled standpoint for modern human beings. In the first place, this position is wrong because, quite simply, it "presupposes that the world does have a meaning" (Weber 1946c

[1917]: 153). By meaning, Weber refers not to the existential effort of individual interpretation but to a conception of teleological purpose in the cosmological sense. It is to this he objects, and he does so because it depends upon an empirical acceptance of God. The religious world-view presupposes "that certain 'revelations' are facts . . . and as such make possible a meaningful conduct of life." What Weber objects to is the notion that certain presuppositions "simply must be accepted," that is, accepted without any rational argument (Weber 1946c [1917]: 154). This is the "intellectual sacrifice" that religion demands as its price for providing a meaningful world.

Weber asks how we have moved from such a "meaningful" world to this disenchanted one of rational choice. The answer is his religious sociology. While the existential need for meaning is constant, the intellectual approach to meaning varies. Religious interpretation emerges before nature or society can be rationally explained. It is a way of explaining the "inexplicable" problems of suffering and unfairness. This origin in inexplicability is what leads religions to center on the problem of salvation. It is because empirical explanation is impossible that there emerges the postulate of God. Because God has created the world, our suffering must be according to his design, and we will be saved insofar as we meet his demands.

Weber created the crosscutting ideal types of his religious sociology in order to explain the approaches to salvation – the theodicies – that had evolved in the course of world history. With the typologies mysticism/asceticism and this-worldly/other-worldly, he sought to describe the degree of emotionality as opposed to control that theodicies allowed, and the degree to which the religious organization of thought and emotion was directed towards world transformation or away from it.

In analyzing this sociology of religion, we must never forget that Weber developed a theory of religious evolution in order to explain religion's self-destruction, that is, the movement from religion to empiricist, naturalistic rationality. What is at issue is whether religion forces the individual to become a tool of divine will rather than a vessel, an issue that will become central to understanding domination as well as individuation: Mystic religions, because they make salvation dependent upon possessing – becoming a vessel of – the spirit of God, encourage emotional expression and experience rather than self-control. Ascetic religions insist that human beings are tools, that they must submit to God's will by following certain rules of good conduct. In this way, asceticism encourages self-control and calculation.

Religious history presents a long march away from mystical to ascetic forms of the search for meaning. For the Australian aborigines, the gods were easily available, and the goal of religious life was an experience of oneness through ritual participation. With the development of monotheism, religion is simplified and abstracted. God withdraws from the world, and humans know him less through experience than through written texts. The Jews were the "people of the book"; they could not even know God's name. This thrust towards asceticism constitutes one of the fundamental causes of the rationalization of religious life. It promotes depersonalization, an outward rather than an inward orientation, and discipline of the self. Though the teleological structure of meaning remains intact, within its confines there has been significant rationalization.

The movement beyond the religious worldview cannot be understood without tracing the implications of Weber's second typology. Early mysticism was almost entirely this-worldly, but later mysticism, Hinduism for example, had a strikingly other-worldly component. For their part, the major ascetic religions had been, until the Reformation, almost entirely other-worldly. They placed their great virtuosi outside the world – for example, in the monasteries of Buddhist and Christian monks. In this earlier period of religious history, renunciation could occur only if ascetics were physically separated from the world. This constituted a tremendous barrier against the spread of rationality.

With the Reformation, all this changed. Ascetic religion, and the rationalizing characteristics it represented, was brought deeply into the world. To achieve salvation, one had to organize the world in accord with the impersonal word of God. This required tremendous depersonalization and self-control. Everything in the world of nature, self, and society had now to be transformed in accordance with God's will. But for this transformation to happen, the whys and the whats would have to be strictly and accurately calculated. Feelings must be renounced in order to estimate God's will in a rational way. Indeed, given the awesome abstraction of God, Puritans could be certain their calculations were rational only if the transformation of this world has actually occurred. The Puritans would be known by their works. Their calling was to master the world.

The stage was now set for the transition to the modern era. This-worldly asceticism continued to permeate the world, but its religious content faded away. The great Protestant scientists – Newton, for example – did not secularize nature in a literal sense. Still, from their commitment to seeing in nature the manifestation of God's will to acting upon it through calculation of its laws was but a small step. Puritan emphasis on the reason of nature and its accessibility to human calculation led directly to the notion of natural law. Natural law allowed causality to be assessed in mechanical terms. True, such anti-metaphysical explanation remained in the service of teleology, but it maintained that no force outside of nature – nothing metaphysical – could govern what was contained within it. Science, and modern rationality more generally, represents the Puritan obsession with calculation, impersonal rules, and self-discipline without the Puritan belief in their divine origin. It is Puritan epistemology without Puritan ontology.

When a calculating and ascetic consciousness comes to dominate the world without being anchored in metaphysics, the result is a sense of meaninglessness. Once the anchor has been dispensed with, human existence seems disorderly, tossed this way and that. Weber (1946c [1917]: 140) writes that the post-religious understanding of life can be only "provisional, not definitive." Rational truth is still pursued, but it becomes cognitively specialized, separated from ultimate values and from other significances. For the Greeks, the exact opposite was the case. They occupied a transitional niche between religion and secular thought, much like the Puritans. Greek science, it was widely believed at the time, could give guidance in all the essentials of life.

If one only found the right concept of the beautiful, the good, or, for instance of bravery, of the soul, one would also grasp its true being. And this, in turn, seemed to open the way for knowing and for teaching how to act rightly in life and, above all, how to act as a citizen of the state. (Weber 1946c [1917]: 141)

But once science separated from metaphysics, rationality can describe only what is, not what ought to be. In this sense it is meaningless, for it cannot answer "the only question important to us," writes Weber, quoting Tolstoy: "'What shall we do and how shall we live?'" This is true, moreover, not only for natural science, but for every form of knowledge that seeks to be rational. Consider aesthetics. "The fact that there are works of art is given for aesthetics," Weber argues. "While it seeks to find out under what conditions this fact exists . . . it does not raise the question whether or not the realm of art is perhaps a realm of diabolical grandeur." Aesthetics does not, in other words, ask the normative question, "should there be works of art?" (Weber 1946c [1917]: 144). Or take jurisprudence. "It establishes what is valid according to the rules of juristic thought," but it never asks "whether there should be law and whether one should establish just these rules." To do the latter would be to assume the meaningfulness of law in a teleological way. The same goes for the historical and cultural sciences. They teach us how to understand and interpret, but "they give us no answer to the question, whether the existence of these cultural phenomena have been and are worthwhile" (Weber 1946c [1917]: 145).

This compartmentalization of rationality has fragmented the once integrated universe. Where once there was security and direction, there is now a metaphysical disorder that gives little solace. "So long as life remains immanent and is interpreted in its own terms," Weber believes, "it knows only of an unceasing struggle of these gods with one another" (Weber 1946c [1917]: 152). Though he senses keenly what has been lost, Weber does not wish that religious cosmology be reconstructed again. He accepts its loss as the price of freedom. This-worldly asceticism has produced a fragmented world without any metaphysical integration, but it is precisely this lack of metaphysical anchorage that throws the individual back upon himself. Once God directed the human person; now the person chooses her gods: "You serve this god and you offend the other god when you decide to adhere to [a] position" (Weber 1946c [1917]: 151).

Rationalization as Domination

Yet, while Weber revered the hard-won autonomy of the modern individual, he did not see individualism as the single defining trait of the twentieth century. Metaphysical nostalgia was far from the only threat to individuality. Against the individual stood barriers of much more material shape. These were the "hard and cold" institutions of the modern world. Even while rationalization stripped illusions and created the possibility for active and mastering behavior, it created the psychological and cultural basis for an extensive institutional coercion that threatened to make freedom a bitter joke. The very forces that free humanity allow it to become dominated in turn. This is the ominous insight with which Weber chose to conclude *The Protestant Ethic and the Spirit of Capitalism*. "The Puritan wanted to work in a calling," he rued (Weber 1958 [1904–5]: 181); "we are forced to do so."

Weber's emphasis in this famous sentence on the voluntariness of the Puritan calling is ambiguous. Referring to the individuating effects of Protestant self-control on the one hand, it points to how asceticism facilitates spiritual and material domination on the other. Hence the sentence that follows: "For when asceticism was carried out of monastic cells into everyday life, and began to dominate worldly morality, it did its part in building the tremendous cosmos of the modern economic order" (Weber 1958 [1904–5]: 181). Demands for large-scale organization have, of course, existed from the beginning of time. Efficiency creates functional reasons for the development of such organization, and the transhistorical human desire for domination creates the psychological fuel. But the culture and psychology of this-worldly asceticism have allowed such "natural" factors to be rationalized in an unprecedented way.

Theoretical blind spots in Weber's work made it virtually impossible for him to carry forward this "other side" of his religious-evolution argument in a consistent way. Weber showed a persistent inability to relate his historical political sociology to the cultural analysis of his religious work (Alexander 1983a), and this is precisely what would have been necessary if this "other side" were to have been revealed in a systematic way. For us to do so here, moreover, would be digressive, for it involves the systematic incorporation of other theoretical traditions.[3] Yet while this other side is never spelled out, the main outlines of what such an argument would be like seem clear enough. The manner in which Weber constructed his historical sociology, the very nature of the categories he chose, convinces us that the outline for this other side was there – in his head, so to speak – even if he was unable to make it explicit or systematically to carry it out. What follows, then, is a post hoc reconstruction of what I would take this theory to be.

Weber believed that this-worldly asceticism made it possible not only to master the world but to master other human beings. Depersonalization and self-discipline promoted autonomy, in part because they allowed actors distance from emotional dependency. But this rejection of one's own dependency needs forced one to reject the needs of others as well. The capacity to make a "tool" out of oneself, therefore, also allowed one to depersonalize and objectify others. Domination could become ruthless only when the personal and idiosyncratic qualities of the other were eliminated. Just as the self became a tool for God, so would others be used for his greater glory. The god of the first great monotheistic religion – the Israelite God Yahweh – was also its god of war, and the very notion of a "just" and crusading war emerged only with Western Judeo-Christianity.

Bureaucracy is the most obvious institutional manifestation of the "other side" of this abstracted, mastering spirit. The Christian Church was the world's first large-scale, successful bureaucracy. The discipline and rationality developed by the monks were important in rationalizing this bureaucracy further, and it was this form of political organization, not only the economic form of capitalism, that later became institutionalized in the world when the metaphysical content of this-worldly asceticism was removed. But economic coercion should not be neglected. Because the Puritans made themselves into tools, they were able to organize others in depersonalized struggle and work. The Puritan objectification of the spirit promoted, in this way, not only economic individualism but the subjective conditions for methodical domination in business and factory.

Politics was transformed in much the same way. Activism and individuality were certainly fundamental to democratization, and Weber himself wrote that religious "election" could be viewed as an incipient form of democracy. Yet, as Weber demonstrated at great length in "Politics as a Vocation," the discipline that underlay modernity would much more likely have the effect of turning political parties, the vehicles for mass political participation, into organizations resembling machines. To produce votes, citizens in a mass society become tools, and modern politics comes to embody the domination and depersonalized motivation left over from asceticized religious life. Even the universities and the enterprises of modern science, institutions that embody more than any other the rational promise of secularizing change, were subject, in Weber's mind, to this transvaluation of values. Chance rather than merit now governs academic advancement (Weber 1946c [1917]: 131–2), and the centralization of research is proletarianizing scientists, turning them into mere cogs in the scientific machine.

Even when he indicated this other side of religious rationalization, Weber did not entirely ignore its benefits, which were not just economic growth and political efficiency but also, paradoxically, equality. The objectification that made people into tools of God's will made them all equally so. The domination of impersonal rules reduced all persons to the same status. As Weber demonstrated in *The City*, citizenship was the other face of depersonalized domination. But outside of this historical essay, he rarely acknowledged that the cultural and psychological capacity for citizenship should lead to political activism and democratic change. He was much more concerned to show how citizenship allowed the mass organization of individuals for demagogic ends.

There is a wide-ranging discussion in Weber's work of the material causes for these new relations of domination. In *Economy and Society*, for example, he conceptualizes the sequence from patriarchal estate to patrimonial/prebendary domination, and he outlines the economic and political exigencies leading from these to modern bureaucratization. The problem with this whole line of discussion (Alexander, 1983a; 1983b), however, is that Weber fails to bring into it the theory of the objectification of the spirit I have just described.

That he knew such a connection existed there seems little doubt. Only the intention to establish such a link can explain the brief, condensed discussion of the relation between charisma and discipline in *Economy and Society*. Weberian interpretation (with the exception of Mitzman 1970) has neatly confined charisma to Weber's typology of political legitimacy and his technical accounts of religious and political innovation. Given Weber's own ambiguity on this point, this is understandable. But it is not correct. There is evidence he tried to utilize the charisma concept more broadly, as the opening for Weber to outline the dark side of spiritual rationalization.

He begins this short segment of *Economy and Society* (Weber 1978: 1148–52) with a general, non-historical statement about charisma and discipline: "It is the fate of charisma to recede before the powers of tradition or of rational association after it has entered the permanent structures of social action." This is simply a restatement of the typology of legitimate domination. What follows, however, shows that Weber has something very different in mind. "The waning of charisma," he writes, "generally indicates the diminishing importance of individual action." But according to the positive side of his rationalization theory – the side that illuminates the development of individuation – rational socialization promotes individual action, not diminishes it. What explains the dramatic shift in Weber's point of view?

Weber wants to point to the fact that rational ideas can work against individualism as well. He stresses that charisma can be the carrier of different kinds of ideas, that it must be treated historically. Of all those powers that lessen the importance of individual action, he writes, "the most irresistible force is rational discipline." In other words, while the waning of charisma always undermines individuality, it does so variably. When it is the carrier of rationalizing ideas, it does so very forcefully indeed.

41

Weber goes on to connect increasing discipline, not only to rationalizing charisma, but to another key element of religious evolution, namely, to increased equality. It "eradicates not only personal charisma," he writes, "but also stratification by status groups." And in the next sentence he makes the link between subjugation and rationalization as explicit as it can possibly be: "The content of discipline is nothing but the consistently rationalized, methodically prepared and exact execution – of the received order, in which all personal criticism is unconditionally suspended and the actor is unswervingly and exclusively set for carrying out the command."

Weber can now discuss the darker side of Puritan development, for he can show how the religious rationalization it entailed led to increased discipline and not just greater autonomy. "Insofar as discipline appeals to firm ethical motives," Weber suggests, "it presupposes a sense of duty and conscientiousness," and in a parenthetical aside he contrasts "men of conscience" and "'men of honor,' in Cromwell's terms." Rather than entrepreneurial activity, Weber makes war the secular outgrowth of the Protestant ethic. He notes "the sober and rational Puritan discipline [that] made Cromwell's victories possible," and goes on to elaborate the contrasting military styles in technical terms. When Weber talks about routinization here, he is referring not to the economic patterns that result from active religious commitment but to the discipline that remains. What is left after the charismatic phase of Puritanism is the habit of strict obedience.

Weber is giving a fundamentally new twist to his famous Protestant-ethic thesis about the relation between religious development and modern society. He refers to the "disciplinary aspect" of every sphere and every historical period, without specifically tying this aspect to the development of this-worldly asceticism. He talks about "the varying impact of discipline on the conduct of war" and argues that it has had "even greater effects upon the political and social order." Discipline, as the basis of warfare, gave birth to "patriarchal kingship among the Zulus . . . Similarly, discipline gave birth to the Hellenic polls with its gymnasia . . . Military discipline was also the basis of Swiss democracy" (Weber 1978: 1152).

42

In other words, key elements in ancient, pre-Judeo-Christian societies and modern post-Reformation ones alike can be causally linked to charismatically generated subjection: "Military discipline was also instrumental in establishing the rule of the Roman patriciate and, finally, the bureaucratic states of Egypt, Assyria, and modern Europe." Weber goes on pointedly to suggest that "the warrior is the perfect counterpart to the monk," the disciplinary aspect of cultural evolution promoting monasteries as it promoted war. "The garrisoned and communistic life in the monastery," Weber writes, "serves the purpose of disciplining [the monk] in the service of his other-worldly master," and, subjects the monk to "his this-worldly master" as well.

The cultural development of discipline is presented here as an independent variable in human history, a cultural push as important as the evolution towards individuation. Weber can write, for example, that "the emancipation of the warrior community from the unlimited power of the overlord, as evidenced in Sparta through the institution of the Ephors, has proceeded only so far as the interest in discipline has permitted." The only point in Weber's entire corpus where he explicitly suggests a subjective side for his explanation of bureaucracy, he identifies bureaucracy as the "most rational offspring" of discipline.

Weber emphasizes not only that cultural discipline – the "other side" of religious rationalization – creates the desire for voluntary subjection, but that it provides a tool for extra-individual domination as well. While the existence of discipline certainly precedes any particular leader's drive for power, it obviously helps a power-hungry leader to achieve his ends. Would-be demagogues seize on discipline and learn how to turn it to their particular purpose; they make good use of "the rationally calculated optimum of the physical and psychic preparedness of the uniformly conditioned masses." Acknowledging that enthusiasm and voluntary devotion continue to mediate even the most disciplined subjection, Weber insists that "the sociologically decisive points" in such relationships must be connected to the historical rise of discipline and the way it facilitates external domination. The rise of disciplined domination means that such "seemingly imponderable and irrational emotional factors" as enthusiasm and devotion are "in principle, at least, calculated in the same manner as one calculates the yield of coal and iron deposits." Rationalization makes followers much more open to discipline: "Devotion is normally impersonal, oriented toward a purpose, a common cause, a rationally intended goal, not a person as such, however personally tinged devotion may be in the case of a fascinating leader."

When Weber writes that "discipline inexorably takes over ever larger areas as the satisfaction of political and economic needs is increasingly rationalized," and that "this universal phenomenon more and more restricts the importance of charisma and of individually differentiated conduct," his intention is clear. He is arguing that rationalization results not only in increased autonomy, but in the spread of impersonal domination through every sphere of life; increased capacity for this-worldly calculation sustains individuation but it simultaneously facilitates subjection and domination.

Weber invented the concept of rationalization to explain the seemingly irreconcilable qualities of the twentieth century. It is not simply the technical growth of military and industrial power that explains the horrors of our time. Dehumanization is a learned, subjective capacity. It develops alongside the capacity for objectification and is generated by the same capacity for depersonalization of other and self. It promotes discipline and subjection, on the one hand, and mastery and autonomy, on the other. With this new understanding, Weber has translated his personal meditation on the human condition into a profound sociology of modern life.[4]

Flights from Rationalization

His personal protestation to the contrary, Weber's social theory does address the question "How should we live?" He conceptualized the moral and emotional implications of the paradox of rationalization in existentialist terms. Like Sartre's reflections in *Being and Nothingness* (1956 [1943]), the pathos of Weber's account derives from his belief in the individual capacity for freedom, though Weber describes this capacity as resulting from historical conditions rather than from human ontology.

In Sartre's trenchant account of human existence (1956 [1943]), the individual faces an inert external world. Inside of the self, the actor experiences cowardly cravings for objectification and release. Both internal and external forces threaten to turn the individual into a thing. The self-consciousness that allows freedom and action becomes a self-objectification that converts contingency into determinism and consciousness into being.

Weber's understanding is remarkably similar. According to his historical understanding, individuality is sociology not ontology, and he sees some degree of objectification as the basis of freedom. But the structures that exist outside Weber's "self" are just as inert, forming an iron cage of depersonalized domination. And the dangers that exist inside of Weber's "self" are just as real. The ego which Weber describes as the proud product of rationalization must contend with its own capacity for self-mortification and its puerile desire to submit to discipline. For Weber, too, this dangerous and unstable situation marks the existential condition of the modern world.

What can an individual do? Weber precedes this question with another. He asks, what is the individual likely to do? Sartre believes that the pressures of existence push the individual towards some mode of flight. One way or another, most people find ways to deny their freedom. They may give up the anguish of being a free person for the horror of viewing themselves as a determined one, constituting their selves as enslaved to external, inhuman force. Or they may engage in play-acting, wrapping themselves in sentimental fantasy and denying the threatening qualities of the world. Both responses are acts of bad faith – escapes from freedom.

Weber also explores flights from the world at length, characterizing them as escape routes peculiar to a modern society. He, too, analyses such flights in terms of pressures from without or within. Though never elaborated as an explicit theory, these late reflections on modernity can be reconstructed as a typology of world-flights. On the basis of this model, I believe, a clear account can be given of Weber's moral prescription for "modern man."

Weber describes a constant tendency for cynical adaptation to the demands of the day. Here is the bureaucrat who obediently follows his orders; the practical politician who pleads his helplessness before interest-group demands and the pressures of the moment; the scientist who becomes a cog in the research machine. In this mode of flight the individual becomes a mere tool of the disciplined spirit; she is no more than a means for some other determinate power or end. Flight from the world can also take an internal form. Rather than accepting the "reality" of her objectified position, the individual tries to recreate oneness with the world, the cosmological experience of pre-modernity. This internal flight takes two forms. It might involve the attempt to re-divinize the world. In this situation, the individual tries to replace the warring gods with a single, all-powerful one that provides a firm, all-encompassing meaning for the world. Here is the idealist, reality-denying politician of "conviction"; the professor who pretends that science can discover the meaning of life and manipulates her position of scientific authority to impart this ultimate meaning to her students; the believer who thinks he has heard the clarion call of modern-day prophecy.

Yet, the re-creation of oneness need not take on this kind of metaphysical hue. It can play out on the psychological level as a commitment to "experientialism" (Weber 1946b [1917]: 340–58). The person aims here to deny the status of "tool" bequeathed by asceticism, to recover the status of "vessel" allowed by mysticism (see Schluchter 1984). Eroticism is one such escape. Sex is pursued for its own sake and comes to constitute the principal meaning of life. Aestheticism is another mystical form of escape; art is experienced as form alone, quite apart from its ethical or intellectual meanings.

Sartre's analysis of flight was abstract and philosophical. Weber's is historical and concrete. With it, he typified unrelenting pathologies of modern times, from the destructive addictions and fantasies of private life to the totalitarian temptations and murderous dictatorships that have marked the public world. He developed a prospective typology of the horrors of the twentieth century, and systematically related it to a vast reconstruction of institutional and cultural history. Perhaps because Weber's world-historical theory of discipline was so little developed, the far-reaching insights of his "flight" theory has never been appreciated. In my view, it constitutes his most important meditation on modern subjectivity.

But Weber is not satisfied, even with this. Just as Sartre insists that bad faith cannot obliterate the freedom that is at the ontological base of the human condition, so Weber rejects the notion that world-flight is inevitable. Morally repulsed by world-flight, he wishes to lay out an alternative. For Sartre, one must accept the anguish of freedom. Weber's answer is not different, but more sociological: one must find a vocation.

Existential Courage and "Vocation"

With the notion of vocation, elaborated primarily in the two essays bearing that title written towards the end of his life, Weber recalls a central theme from his analysis of cultural development in the pre-secular age. It was Luther who first emphasized the *Beruf*, and the Puritans who first made the "calling" central to religious salvation. The Puritans' vocation represented the first and most important result of the turn towards this-worldly asceticism, the religious movement that so decisively supported the development of rationality and individuation even while it ushered in the forces that threatened to overwhelm both reason and the individual.

To practice a vocation as the Puritans did means to be disciplined by a moral spirit that facilitates the realization of the self. In the first place, therefore, it is to avoid the mystical experientialism that represents a major flight from reality in the modern world. Vocational commitment also prevents the cynical adaptation to external conditions that self-objectification and material domination can beget. Finally, the Puritan vocation, while definitely a conviction, was not an idealistic commitment in the utopian sense of world-flight. Vocational conviction accepts the limits of the division of labor and institutional rationalization; its moral discipline is narrowed to the requirements of a specific task.

In all these ways, I believe, Weber was convinced that the ancient vocation of the Puritans and the contemporary vocation of modern men and women are the same, yet Weber saw an enormous difference as well.[5] The Puritans maintained their vocation in the service of God, their convictions and works serving to maintain the fabric of cosmological meaning. The modern vocation cannot allow such an intellectual sacrifice if the fruits of rationalization are maintained. Once this-worldly asceticism escaped from the cosmological net, it allowed a radically new form of autonomy and self-control. This-worldly religious asceticism created the first opportunity for vocation, but only in post-religious society could the vocational commitment achieve a liberating, existentialist form. Weber believes that vocational morality allows modern persons to maintain their autonomy in the face of the objective pressures of the iron cage.

The language Weber uses to describe vocation in contemporary society makes this link between Puritan and modern vocation unmistakably clear. The similarity in discourse demonstrates that secular vocations can allow some of the same psychological and cultural satisfactions as religious life. Science, Weber writes, can become an "*inward* calling" (Weber 1946c [1917]: 134, emphasis in original) whose significance for the practitioner touches the most profound issues of existence: "Whoever lacks the capacity to . . . come up to the idea that the fate of his soul depends upon whether or not he makes the correct conjecture at this passage of this manuscript may as well stay away from science" (Weber 1946c [1917]: 135). Vocation, then, is concerned with salvation in the deepest sense of the word. It connects the "soul" of "modern man" – which evidently Weber thinks still exists – to rationalized tasks in the modern world. The experience of a vocation can even be mystical in a secular way, though the passion it inspires and the "strange intoxication" it affords may be "ridiculed by outsiders." Vocational commitment allows the experience of perfection associated with being a mystical vessel of God: "The individual can acquire the sure consciousness of achieving something truly perfect in the field of science" (Weber 1946c [1917]: 134). To have such a calling is to realize the great humanistic ideals, "for nothing is worthy of man as man unless he can pursue it with passionate devotion" (Weber 1946c [1917]: 135).

48

The same possibility for maintaining "rational religion" is held out in Weber's politics essay. Here, too, Weber wants to suggest that the result of this-worldly asceticism need not be self-mortification and the crushing discipline of external force. Here, too, he presents this argument by using religious language in a secular way. Politics, of course, is intimately associated with violence. At first, this association was mitigated by the degree to which politicians could live "for" politics, maintaining, thereby, some sense of individual responsibility and control. But with mass democracy, the need develops to organize and discipline the masses, and the mass politician learns to live "off" politics. The ideal type of this new politician, the man without a vocation for politics, is the boss, the "absolutely sober man" (Weber 1946a [1917]: 109) who embodies the flight from rationalization typified as cynical adaptation to the demands of the day.

It is the rudderless man without the calling for politics who produces the "soullessness" of modern politics. But this situation is not inevitable. There remains the possibility for "'innerly' called" leaders (Weber 1946a [1917]: 79). To have a calling, the politician must subject self to the discipline of a moral cause – "the serving of a cause must not be absent if action is to have inner strength" (Weber 1946a [1917]: 117). The exact nature of the cause is a matter of individual choice, but "some kind of faith must always exist." But commitment to a cause must remain secular if it is not to reflect the search for re-divinization that represents another flight from the world. If politicians were to submit to such an essentially religious point of view, they would be committed not to a vocation but to an ethic of ultimate ends, to the "politics of conviction." What Weber advocates instead is the "ethic of responsibility."

Responsible, vocational political ethics can be achieved only if moral commitment is disciplined by rational assessment of realistic possibilities for gaining one's ideals. "One has to give an account of the foreseeable results of one's action" (Weber 1946a [1917]: 120). Faith, then, need not be eliminated from modern politics, but it must be disciplined by rationality. "It takes both passion and perspective," Weber writes (Weber 1946a [1917]:

128). "What is decisive," he insists, is not only idealistic commitment but "the trained relentlessness in viewing the realities of life" (Weber 1946a [1917]: 126–7). Adding such scientific realism to faith, of course, is precisely what pushes this-worldly asceticism to individuation rather than cosmology, and it is this demand for "rational accounting" that makes the pressure on the post-cosmological individual so much more intense. What becomes decisive in achieving individuation is "the ability to face such realities and to measure up to them inwardly" (Weber 1946a [1917]: 127). Only if this strength is achieved can a person have a calling for politics. Anyone "who is not spiritually dead" must realize that such a possibility does exist.

It is certainly not correct, then, to say, as so many of Weber's interpreters have, that Weber saw no escape from the iron cage other than the pursuit of irrational, charismatic politics. It is no more correct, indeed, than to describe Weber's sociology, as so many also have, as a paean to the realization of individuality in its various forms.[6] Rationalization is a movement towards individuation, but it allows for the conditions of individuality rather than individuality as such, for rationalization also creates the psychological needs and cultural codes that sustain anti-individualistic institutional coercion in turn. Faced with such destructive, depersonalizing forces, the individual either flees from them and gives up independence, or confronts them and maintains it.

Weber presents this confrontation as an existential choice, with all the arbitrariness that such a position implies. Sartre is right to insist that nothing can explain or predict whether an actor has the courage to accept the anguish of freedom. Weber expresses exactly the same sentiment when he suggests that vocational commitment depends on "the ability to face these realities and to measure up to them inwardly." Sartre is convinced that such courage is rarely to be found, and Weber entirely agrees. From *The Protestant Ethic* on, Weber emphasizes just how unlikely vocational behavior in the modern world will be. "The idea of duty in one's calling," he writes, "prowls about in our lives like the ghost of dead religious beliefs" (Weber 1958 [1904–5]: 182). When occupational behavior is disconnected from religious direction or direct economic necessity, he suggests – clearly referring to conditions developing in the twentieth century – it will rarely be elevated to a calling: "Where the fulfilment of the calling cannot directly be related to the highest spiritual and cultural values, or when, on the other hand, it need not be felt simply as economic compulsion, the individual generally abandons the attempt to justify it at all."

Beyond Rationalization Theory: towards a Fuller Dialectic

This sociology of modern life leaves us in a rather uncomfortable position. Weber has described an extraordinary dialectic of individuality and domination, and he has shown how, from this crucible, there emerge the flights from reality and the courageous assertions of freedom that are characteristic markers of our time. Secularization has made freedom a possibility that personal courage can achieve, but it is impossible to predict whether such true individuality will ever be realized. Depersonalization is also an undeniable, profoundly disturbing fact of modern life. The twentieth century was strewn with societies brutalized by technology, choked by totalitarianism, and sapped by existential flight.

Yet for all its breathtaking illumination – and Weber achieved more clarity about the dangers of modernity than any theorist before or since – this understanding does not seem entirely satisfactory.

The course of modernity has, indeed, been marked by dreadful self-enslavement,[7] but it has also been the site of extraordinary breakthroughs in rational understanding of mental life and democratic support of individual rights, breakthroughs that have bolstered the self in turn.[8] While every society has been weakened by individual and group flights from reality and crippled by hierarchical domination, societies have also managed acute crises and chronic strains in ways that have allowed them to sustain reasonable patterns of life. Even societies that succumbed to the horrors of modernity contained movements and institutions of a more rational and responsive bent, and the forms of organization that emerged from their destruction demonstrated that "rational learning" can take place on a societal scale.

51

Weber's sociology indicates that in modernity destructive moments can be overcome, but it does not explain how. The overcoming has not been random, nor has it depended on the contingency of individual courage alone. There were structural reasons which can be sociologically explained (see chapter 8, below).

Weber argued that scientific rationality and ethical values should coexist, but he did not identify the conditions under which such a coexistence might be achieved. Durkheim did just that. He did so by producing a systematic argument for the continuing "religious" needs of human beings, needs that explain the construction of secular symbol systems that continually transform them at the same time. Durkheim knew that it is not simply individual courage and existential contingency that permit modern persons to go beyond the purely rationalistic stance of science. Like Weber, he considered it inevitable that rational knowledge would be experienced as radically incomplete. The search for non-rational meaning, however, was not considered by Durkheim as something that could be conducted in an entirely individualistic way.

Not only flights from reality but attempts to confront it ethically are sustained, according to late-Durkheimian sociology, by supra-individual, group processes. Even science, Durkheim came to believe, must be viewed in such group terms. Science is accepted to the degree that the value of critical rationality becomes part of both the structures of modern society and the belief systems of human beings. Modern social systems can allow social movements to sacralize "rational," emancipatory values, that confront domination.

In this chapter, I have explained that Weber was hardly blind to such positive possibilities. He who wrote about vocational commitments acknowledged that some political leaders live for politics rather than off it. In an important early essay (Weber 1985; Alexander and Loader 1985), he suggested that participatory democracy might be sustained in nations that had experienced sect rather than church religion. Weber outlined a theory of citizenship for the early modern period, and he acknowledged that the formal abstractions of modern law could be abrogated by oppressed groups seeking substantive rationality.

Weber saw that religious evolution had freed the individual in modern societies, but he described this modern individual as isolated and culturally abandoned. Depersonalization had changed institutional structures in a positive way, but it left a coercive institutional residue and its socialized motivations remained dangerously dependent.

— 3 —

BARBARISM AND MODERNITY: EISENSTADT'S REGRET

Modern societies in the twentieth century first fissured, then shattered, into the warring camps of liberal democracy, communist revolution, and fascist reaction. So did modern intellectuals. These intellectual and social divisions were hardly unrelated. In fact, the social divisions can be framed, and sometimes were inspired by, the theoretical reflections of Marx, Nietzsche, and Weber.

The terms of this fateful conflict can be conceived as different answers to the question that has been asked many times and in many different ways: Is the universalism and abstraction that characterizes modern life good or bad?

Modernity has encased human action and institutions with abstract ethical demands and impersonal requirements – from moral and secular law to the rule of expert advice, from income tax to bureaucratic controls, from market exigencies and currency adjustments to psychotherapy, from surveillance to democratic control, from peaceful coexistence under international statutes and laws to stand-offs and armed confrontation, tense vigilance, and techno-war.

Can this kind of abstraction and impersonality be lived with? Can it be user friendly? Does it contribute to reform, to humanism, to justice, and inclusion? Does it make people fulfilled, authentic, or even just plain happy? Does it make them civilized?

The answers to these fundamental questions have been "yes," "not right now but someday soon, if we do something radical," and "never."

The "yes" answer is what Parsons took from Weber (Parsons 1973).[1] The transcendentalism of the radical Protestant tradition has issued in liberal democracy, which is rule bound in a good way. The scientific revolution was a great step forward, and it promoted a form of objective truth seeking that allowed social problems to be evaluated and alleviated. The modern personality is protean and capable, and handles this new discipline in an autonomous manner. Barbarism can only be a product of premodern societies; in modernity, therefore, barbarism results from the primordial residues of earlier life. Modern abstraction, autonomy, and discipline supply the resources, and also the will, for a civilizing process that institutionalizes idealistic utopias in this-worldly form.

The second response – "not right now but someday soon, if we do something radical" – is what left-wing revolutionaries have answered. Everything liberals say is true, but only up to a point. What they have not realized is that the great energy and bounty of civilization leads not only to objectification in the good sense – as in Hegel's *Phenomenology*, where it produces emotional and moral growth – but in the bad sense as well. Objectification in modern societies produces alienation in Marx's sense, reification in Lukács' (Lukács 1971 [1924]). There is a dialectic of the enlightenment, such that inequality and oppression come out of modernity, and not primarily freedom and solidarity (Horkheimer and Adorno 1969). The latter are only for the dominant and privileged classes; the former are the lot of most humankind. So the modern age produces turmoil and strife, not amelioration and equilibrium. But history also provides an opportunity to overcome this ambiguous legacy of the Axial Age, so that it can be made good. The Puritans of old, under the yoke of modern abstraction, made capitalism and bourgeois democracy. Bearing the same cultural and organizational burden, the new Puritans – Marxists, Leninists, Maoists – would create communism and workers' democracy. Revolution is this-worldly asceticism in our own time (Eisenstadt 1978). The result will be a just order. The deracinating promise of bourgeois modernity will finally be fulfilled in the next historical time.

The third response to the basic question is "No;" modernity, *tout court*, simply is not a good thing. The abstraction that humans are bound to live with is fundamentally "other," and unbearable for that. It sets up tensions that tear people away from themselves. The passions of human nature cannot be corrected or civilized through abstract morality, the hypocrisies of which they must be fundamentally in rebellion against (Nietzsche 1956 [1872, 1887]). Modernity unleashes, not enlightenment, but an even darker dark age. It cannot be saved through disciplined revolution, which would only make it worse. It must be discarded.

Some critics have argued that an alternative to modernity can be found by just saying no, by taking the route of other-worldly or this-worldly mysticism (Roszack 1969; Alexander 2000b). Others have insisted that modernity must be destroyed by violence, of a right-wing not a left-wing form.[2] Both kinds of critics agree that a new world can set aside the tensions of the Axial Age. Unity can be restored. Depending on which path to restoration is chosen, there will be concreteness, not abstraction; release, not discipline; fusion, not division; play, not work. Only if abstract morality and inner-worldly discipline are set aside will humans be able to lead a truly human life.[3]

The historically specific conflicts in which these three answers were encoded during the twentieth century apparently have come to an end. It seems unlikely that communist and fascist revolutions will rise again as alternative answers to the question of modernity, at least in the forms that are horrifically familiar to us today (Furet 1999). But, despite the escatological expectations of "1989," it has also become clear that the more fundamental arguments over modernity remain. From postmodern nihilism to antimodern fundamentalism, there is still basic disagreement over the question of modernity, and the radical alternatives to liberal democracy remain robust if less ideologically coherent.

Eisenstadt's sociology allows us to frame this ontological anxiety of modernity in an historical way. In his theory of the Axial Age, he explained that "fundamental contradictions" are immanent to modernity, tensions that cannot ever be resolved and which take different social forms depending on the balance of forces at hand (Eisenstadt 1982; Alexander 1992b: 85–94). These tensions reach their greatest intensity in Western modernity, where this-worldly asceticism first had its day, but they were characteristic of every religious civilization created in the Axial Age. The Axial Age marked a sharp break from the unified cosmos, or at least from the more incrementally stratified cosmos and social structure of archaic religious and social life. It established a sharp and unbridgeable break between the heavenly, ideal world and the mundane social sphere inhabited by merely human beings. Especially in what became known as the Western tradition, not only the Judaic-Christian but the Greek, this break took especially severe and radical forms. Rituals were attacked as making things too easy. Salvation became a serious problem, and grace often an unattainable, even unfathomable, goal. Human beings were submitted to harsh judgments from a righteous and wrathful god. Judged by a powerful and distant divinity, humans learned to judge themselves in an equally unforgiving way (Weber 1958 [1904–5]). Donning Rawls' "veil of ignorance," men and women submit to Kant's categorical imperative.

The social results of this-worldly asceticism, whether religious or secular, are there for all to see. The Calvinists created not only capitalism but radical democracies – Walzer's revolutionary saints, Eisenstadt's puritan-like Jacobins (Walzer 1965; Eisenstadt 1999). This duality, with its guilty demand to find grace via this-worldly action, made Westerners into world transformers, history's greatest empire builders, whose dominion spread far beyond the West to transform and "modernize" the entire world (Eisenstadt 1987).[4]

For liberal moderns, the tensions and opportunities of Axial civilization continue to mark the vital characteristics of the modern age. It helps us to understand the restlessness that surrounds us, the existential demand for self-examination in order to act in good faith and not blame others by shifting responsibilities away from ourselves.[5] It explains the need for continuous discipline and achievement, and the feeling that charisma can never be fully institutionalized (Eisenstadt 1968a: 167–201). Grace is available, but it can't be bottled, even if it can be sold.

But we are not only liberal moderns. There is a persistent unease with civilization (Freud 1961 [1930]), and there are different answers to the question of modernity first posed by the Axial Age. There is a dark side of Axial Age theory that needs to be pressed much further, a weakness in the structure and culture of modern societies that has not been sufficiently plumbed, much less system-atically explored. Does the separated ideal posited by the Webe-rian tradition remain *whole* and *transcendent* in the manner that liberal social theory suggests?

Transcendent. The ability to tie the Axial Age breakthrough to human progress, to the institutionalization of principled ethics and democratic reform, rests on the assumption that human beings can tolerate the tension without flinching or backing away. To many, this assumption seems valid and this ability obvious enough; but Max Weber himself expressed doubts. In "Religious Rejections of the World and Their Directions" (1946b [1917]: 323–59), Weber outlined different kinds of flights from the demands of this-worldly asceticism (see chapter 2, above). Each of these efforts undermined the capacity of ethical judgment to make good on compelling moral obligations. They undermined dualism, providing expressive outlets for symbolic processes that lent them a mystical form. Weber speaks of aestheticism, of art for art's sake, which echoes Nietzsche's rejection of the good for the beautiful and his attack on the sustainability of modern moral claims. Weber also speaks of eroticism, demands for impulse release, and romantic love, whether love for another or for divine representatives of God.

Weber presents a range of forces that undermine discipline and autonomy, tempting moderns into bad faith. They are, in Fromm's words, "escapes from freedom."[6] Every modern person fears that freedom might be too hard, too unkind, too intrinsically unfulfilling. There is some evidence in Weber's writings that he sees this need to escape, not merely as a "micro" problem, or an incidental one, but as a systemic and dangerous macro-social strain. He speaks, for example, of militarism and various forms of popular enthusiasm as providing flights from ascetic discipline that are positively sanctioned by society.[7] It is this strain in his theorizing that explains Weber's attention to plebiscitarian democ-racy, the political populism that offers masses of people the chance to experience the charisma of the demagogue. Weber saw such modern prophets as distorting the Hebraic heritage and feared their great potential for wreaking havoc on the institutions of modern life.

While expressed in a fragmentary manner, Weber's insights into flights from modernity illuminate how difficult it is to maintain transcendental abstraction and moral universalism in the modern world. Illustrations of such flight mark modernity from its beginnings. Consider, for example, the experiments of the Puritan settlers in early America.[8] Despite the fact that their covenant with God made it formally impossible to know whether or not they were saved, the Puritans soon found ways. They established the "half way covenant" to allow their children to be born into the church, to achieve election without having to earn it. They allowed good works to become evidence of good faith, rather than its result. When these Puritan Americans first conceived of themselves as God's chosen people, they understood this status in the covenantal terms of the ancient prophets. Soon, however, it also became a signal of their having *already* been saved. It awarded them a special righteous status that ensured their own goodness as compared with the faithlessness of others. It is hard to continually sit in judgment of one's self. It is much easier to release tension by embracing the innocence of one who is always and already saved.[9]

Wholeness. The flight from transcendence in modern society is also connected to the way abstract and universalistic regulating ethical structures have been continuously polarized. Righteousness has always been defined in connection with wickedness. Goodness has been inseparable from evil (Alexander 2003a). The fundamental fact of this splitting, of this binary thinking, allows us to understand the tension relief, the flight from transcendence that Weber described, in more systematic and theoretically sophisticated ways. In psychoanalytic terms, splitting can be understood in terms of Anna Freud's classical theory of the mechanisms of defense (Freud 1993 [1936]). Unable to stand the anxiety entailed by autonomy and self-control, the ego splits the world and projects the causes of anxiety outside the self, onto others. The stress and strain are out there, not in here; we defend ourselves against internal tension by fighting against these outside threats.

This conceptual language allows us to connect ethical polarization to the flight from transcendence. But there are other theoretical languages that allow us to explain this process in more sociological ways. One is through the theory of social closure, which such thinkers as Dahrendorf (1959), Erikson (1966), Parkin (1979), Lamont (1992), Giesen (1998), and Brubaker (2002) have conceptualized in more instrumental or more cultural ways. Closure theory operationalizes Weber's pessimism via a model of social organization. Every collectivity demands a boundary, creating an inside and outside. Closure applies to small groups, such as sects, but also to larger societies, such as political parties and religions, and to nation-states and civilizations as well.

Closure theory needs to be culturally expanded. Semiotics shows all thinking as binary, all concepts defined by their opposites. The late Durkheim, who inspired Saussure and thus helped father semiotics, put a moral and emotional spin on this understanding (Alexander 1988d; Alexander and Smith 2005). He conceptualized inside and outside as sacred and profane, as right and left sacred, as pure and impure. These ideas were developed by early anthropological theories of pollution and taboo, then by Caillois and Bataille, and later still by Mary Douglas. These thinkers demonstrated that pollution and stigma are fundamental processes in social life, even or perhaps especially in its modern form. This move makes both antagonism and transgression into fundamental processes of modernity (see chapters 5–7 below).

These lines of organizational and cultural thinking clarify, in a theoretical rather than empirical manner, why the beneficent power of ideal regulation that the Axial Age introduced, and modernity promised to perfect, has so continuously been fragmented and brought down to earth. This declension has been fuelled by the energetic obsessions of this-worldly asceticism and by insistent efforts to escape from it. What results is perversion of the ethical demands created by the Axial Age.

It is because transcendence can be so easily undermined and wholeness so consistently broken that modernism and barbarism have been so closely intertwined. We are the righteous ones that God has chosen. They are the evil ones who afflict us, and it is they who are responsible for the troubles we are in today. We are pure; they are polluted. We are innocent; they guilty. Our salvation depends, not on regulating our own desires and actions, but on purifying the outside world of those polluted others. Only by destroying them can we ourselves be saved.

It is no wonder that God's grace has been so hard to find in societies formed by this-worldly asceticism. The search for alternative pathways to (secular) grace has propelled self-defeating revolutionary experiments, of the left and the right. But it has also inspired humanizing kinds of mystical flights. Hinduism and Buddhism have made increasing incursions into the religious life of the Western educated strata (Alexander 2000b; Campbell 2007). New Age movements have reversed Weber's historical preference for instrumental rationality in a more secular way. The deep underground spring that feeds this recent outcropping is romanticism, which at the very beginnings of industrial society made its case that moderns should be vessels rather than merely tools of the divine. From that time on, romanticism, for better and for worse, has been interlarded with ascetic modernity. The ambition of this short chapter has been to suggest why.

— 4 —

INTEGRATION AND JUSTICE:
PARSONS' UTOPIA

Talcott Parsons' approach to what he called the "societal community" sought to connect the claims of social integration and the
possibilities of justice. A good society needs to have community
solidarity. But this community has to be articulated in a manner
that allows its symbols and norms to include every group that is
functionally involved in, or organizationally subject to, the values
and institutions of the social system. If you don't have solidarity,
you do not have the subjective dimension of community. Without
such subjective community, you cannot have feelings of mutual
obligation, and without feelings of obligation there can be no
voluntary assumption of responsibility. Yet, feelings of moral solidarity are not enough, in and of themselves. If the solidary norms
of society are not broad and inclusive, the subjectively powerful
community operates in a limited and excluding way. It will be just.
You can have cultural hegemony without the normative structure
of democracy: integration without justice.

Parsons was not sufficiently attentive to such a distinction
between integration and solidarity, his theoretical and historical
writings on the societal community confusing rather than clarify-
ing their relation. Obscuring the potential conflict between hierarchy and horizontal integration, his writing sometimes suggested
that the "functional" need for hierarchy was more important, even
in moral terms, than the question of whether the members of the
wider society feel solidarity with one another. Parsons' general
theory often sacrificed justice for solidarity. In his empirical

treatments of the contemporary American societal community, however, Parsons actually tended to idealize rather than neglect the connection between integration and justice. He often suggested that in America a nearly perfect blend of social integration and social justice had been achieved.

In this chapter, I suggest that Parsons' evolutionary theory of modernity was an effort to finesse these ambiguities – the theoretical relation between justice and integration, on the one hand, and the empirical relation between the contemporary United States and world history, on the other. That this resolution was not successful, I will demonstrate, is revealed by the train of semantic stuttering that punctuates Parsons' exclamations about America's putatively democratic triumph.

Ambiguity about the relationship between integration and justice was already ensconced at the center of Parsons' theoretical project in his first book, *The Structure of Social Action* (1937). While ostensibly an effort at pure analytic theory, aiming only at interpretation and explanation, *Structure* implicitly addressed issues of democracy, order, and justice raised by the social movements and instabilities of the interwar period. There were two solutions to the "problem of order" in *Structure*, one democratic and critical, the other nondemocratic and conservative. Both solutions derived from Parsons' critique of theories that emphasized instrumental rationality, which he called rationalistic utilitarianism or radical positivism. Instrumental presuppositions about the nature of action, Parsons believed, made it impossible to understand how social order was possible. In his democratic solution to the order problem, Parsons insisted that, insofar as a theory assumed purely instrumental action, it could envision only aggressive, polarizing, and destructive social conflict. Within this framework, the only way to achieve order was to impose it from the outside, as Hobbes had when he argued the necessity of a coercive, antidemocratic *Leviathan*. As an alternative, Parsons recommended that sociological theory step outside of the limiting assumption of instrumental rationality and recognize the centrality to social action of normative orientation. In this manner, a more democratic solution to order would become possible.

According to Parsons, bringing the normative element back in would allow theory to recognize voluntary, self-control. Such voluntaristic control creates an institutional and moral basis for an order that differs from antidemocratic power. In this solution to Hobbes' problem, Parsons followed Locke's own political response to Hobbes' antidemocratic opposition to the English revolution. Parsons acknowledges Locke but only in an analytical, not a normative, sense. Avoiding explicit moral positioning, Parsons follows Halévy's criticism that Lockean political-economy emphasized the natural as compared to the artificial identity of interests. He suggests that a sociological theory of normativity can translate the artificial identity of interest into more realistic (i.e., more institutional) and more democratic terms.

In Parsons' later work – from *The Essays in Sociological Theory* (1954) to *The Social System* (1951), the AGIL model (Parsons and Smelser 1956), and the evolutionary theory (Parsons 1966a, 1973) – one can trace a line of theorizing that builds upon a democratic solution to the order problem. Parsons developed a model of the components of social action and social systems that constitute a continuum from coercive to self-regulating and free (Parsons 1967, and more generally, Parsons 1966a, 1973). This continuum pushed off to one side, and implicitly criticized, the dehumanizing and antidemocratic practices of instrumental rationality and coercion, and pointed to the alternative of what Parsons conceived as cybernetically higher levels of intentional, culturally-guided action and meaningful cooperation. Explicitly, Parsons praised this solution to the problem of order for its efficiency. Relying upon information rather than energy, this more "normative" approach evoked the cybernetic logic that so intrigued many thinkers in the postwar period. Parsons' emphasis on these normative forms of action and order also allowed him to achieve a more ideological purpose. He could promote a social system based on ethical institutions such as law (Parsons 1977) and citizenship (Parsons 1966b), one in which the major media of communication were influence (Parsons 1969a) and value commitments (1969b) rather than power and money. It was this line of thinking that informed the democratic potential of Parsons' societal community idea.[1]

From the very beginning of Parsons' work, however, this critical-democratic line of his thinking was shadowed by a conservative, nondemocratic one. This shadowing began with a different kind of solution to the order problem. In *Structure*, it turns out, Parsons was not only concerned with solving the order problem in a voluntaristic manner. He often suggested the problem with Hobbes' *Leviathan* was not its antidemocratic ethics but its empirical weakness. External force did not solve the order problem well enough. To be effective in curbing chaos and anomie, social order needed an internal reference; it would have to work upon an actor's subjectivity. Internal order can be altered only through norms, for, in contrast with material organization, norms can be internalized.

According to this minimalist perspective, normative order is more efficient, not more just. Normative order per se is not democratic; it is merely cultural. If cultural control is powerful enough, it can achieve integration, inducing internally generated cooperation, consensus, and agreement. Yet, such integration will be mere hegemony, in Gramsci's pejorative sense, if it does not also define democratic alternatives, normatively emphasizing pluralism, criticism, and universalism. The minimalist solution to the order problem has the latent effect, in other words, of substituting integration for justice, a displacement that has been central to conservative, antidemocratic thinking whose animus is revolution and disorder. If stability is all that matters, any normative framework will do. It need not be the sort of normative framework that promotes justice.

To make integration and stability so central is to sacrifice justice. While the central tenets of justice are equality and recognition, the search for justice often leads to conflict, increasing rather than decreasing disorder and immediate social strain. Adhering to democratic forms of normative order often produces intense dissatisfaction and conflict. There is an endemic strain between the idealized implications of a normative order and its particular institutionalization in historically specific social systems. If norms are to inspire self-criticism and reflexivity, and to motivate and legitimate demands for justice, they must reach beyond equilibrium to social conflict and change. The institutionalization of a normative order may lead to trust in the ideals that anchor a system while delegitimating those who hold authoritative positions and the organizations they support (Barber 1983).

Ambiguous Definitions of Societal Community

This ambivalence about order and normativity is inflected in Parsons' foundational definitions of societal community. In the following, I deconstruct two of these, differentiating the key statements in each discussion by number and the key propositions within each statement by letter. Parsons' original statements are in italics. My glosses follow the italics in roman type. I draw here from *Societies: Evolutionary and Comparative Perspectives* (1966), where Parsons first introduced the concept of societal community.

1. *[a] The core of a society . . . is the patterned normative order through which the life of a population is collectively organized. [b] As an order, it contains values and differentiated and particularized norms . . . As a collectivity, it displays a patterned conception of membership, [c] which distinguishes between those individuals who do and do not belong. (1966: 10)*
    1a: Parsons introduces here the distinction between the core of a society and the population at large. Whether he means to identify the core with a particular group or with the center in a more metaphorical sense, it is clear that Parsons equates this core with both the normative order and the collective, non-normative organization of the life of the population. By the life of the population, Parsons means to include individuals and groups who are administratively or functionally part of the social system but who are outside the core.
    1b: While the normative dimension of order refers to values that in principle can be shared across groups, the organizational dimension of collectivity defines membership in a manner that may confine the enforcement of normative meanings to members of a particular group.
    1c: Membership defines those who are inside and outside the organized collectivity.
2. *[a] Problems involving the "jurisdiction" of the normative system may make impossible an exact coincidence between the status of "coming under" normative obligations and the status of membership, [b] because the enforcement of a normative system seems inherently linked to the control (e.g., through the "police function") of sanctions*

66

[c] exercised by and against the people actually residing within a territory. (ibid.)

2a: Those who are expected to adhere to the normative order may not actually be considered members of the society to which this normative order is considered to apply.

2b: There is a difference between the symbolic reach of a normative order and its enforcement. Enforcement involves complex organizational sanctions and often coercion, as the nearly universal existence of a policing apparatus suggests.

2c: People may be part of a society's territory, that is, part of the "life of the population," even if they are excluded from membership, and thus be subject to a society's coercive sanctions. This application of coercion may be authorized by one segment of the population, generally the core members, against another segment whose members do not voluntarily accept the dominant normative order in a subjective sense and are not allowed to become members of it.

3. *[a] We will call this one entity of the society . . . the societal community . . . It is constituted both by a normative system of order and by statuses, rights and obligations pertaining to membership [b] which may vary for different sub-groups within the community. [c] To survive and develop, the social community must maintain the integrity of a common cultural orientation, broadly (though not necessarily uniformly or unanimously) shared by its membership, as the basis of its societal identity. (ibid.)*

3a: The societal community is that part of the normatively defined community that establishes collective membership. Such membership may be attenuated in various ways.

3b: There are subgroups in a social system which do not have full membership in the societal community.

3c: The normative element of the society defining its collective identity is the culture shared by its core group members.[2]

These difficult passages point to the tension between Parsons' interest in integration and justice. Parsons believes that his concept of societal community can reconcile these concerns, but it becomes rough going when he confronts the fragmentation of actually existing empirical societies. Despite his clear stress on the integrating nature of societal community, Parsons is compelled to acknowledge, not only the existence of subgroups that segment actually existing social systems, but the fact that, because of such divisions, the norms of a binding community are not likely to cover the entire population of a given territory. The reason Parsons offers for this alarming fact is that the normative reach of cultural values exists in tension with the realistic possibility of their enforcement. Norms do not only create moral integration but also define membership, deciding who is in and who out. The norms defining the culture of the societal community might refer to everybody who occupies a territory – the "life of the population." There are subgroups inside this population, however, who may not actually be members of the community. For them, integration is not voluntary but coerced; they "come under" the norms, but may not accept them. In this case, cooperation can be secured only by police power, by repression rather than influence and normative control.

Parsons implicitly acknowledges here that the societal community may not be integrative for society in general but only for its core group. This possibility makes manifest that integration and justice are empirically unrelated. Rather than combating exclusion, the societal community might actually produce it. This emphatically is not the way Parsons himself presents the case. He makes it seem as if the integrative impulse of norms would embrace the community *if only* the police function didn't get in the way. If ever there were a residual category, however, this is it. Policing is not just a functional requisite of society. It develops also in response to the strains between those who are members and those who are not, from the efforts of the former to protect their identity and interest from the latter.

The same systemic ambiguity about the relation between integration and justice afflicts Parsons' second major treatment of societal community, *The System of Modern Societies* (1973). While the empirical reference for the 1966 book *Societies* considered societal community in simple, archaic, and "seed bed" societies, the later treatment brings the concept into contact with more recent Western history, from medieval society to more or less the present day. Despite its different empirical material, the later treatment reproduces the tensions in Parsons' earlier discussions.

1. *[a] Because we treat the social system as integrative for action systems generally, we must pay special attention to the ways in which it achieves – or fails to achieve – various kinds of levels of internal integration. We will call the integrative subsystem of a society the societal community. Perhaps the most general function of a societal community is to articulate a system of norms with a collective organization that has unity and*

cohesiveness . . . [b] The collective aspect is the societal community as a single, bounded, collectivity. Social order requires clear and definite integration in the sense, on the one hand, of normative coherence and, on the other hand, of societal "harmony" and "coordination" . . . [c] The primary function of this integrative subsystem is to define the obligations of loyalty to the societal collectivity, both for the membership as a whole and for various categories of differentiated status . . . [d] In its hierarchical aspect, the normative ordering of the societal community in terms of memberships comprises its stratification scale, the scale of the accepted . . . prestige of subcollectivities, statuses, and roles and of persons as societal members. It must be coordinated . . . with universal norms governing the status of membership. (1973: 11–12)

1a: Societal community is explicitly identified with integration in the sense of stability, unity, and homogeneity.

1b: The scope of normative integration is equated with a bounded and organized collectivity.

1c: Normative integration is about loyalty, not criticism; those excluded from the organized collectivity are expected to be loyal to the norms of the membership community.

1d: There are degrees of membership even within the societal community itself. Via prestige rankings, normative integration is adapted to the vertical imperative of stratification, allocating the qualities that define the core group to those who are most fully its members. More universalistic norms of membership might conflict with this stratificational dimension of normative order.

2. *[a] A society must constitute a societal community that has an adequate level of integration or solidarity and a distinctive membership status. [b] This does not preclude relations of control or symbiosis with population elements only partially integrated into the societal community, such as the Jews in the Diaspora, but there must be a core of fully integrated members. (ibid., p. 17)*

2a: The societal community is that core part of the social system that has a distinctive membership and achieves integration and solidarity.

2b: Solidarity and integration of the core group can exist side by side with coercive control exercised by the core group over excluded members. The achievement of solidarity is not mitigated by the existence of such repression.

Resolving Ambiguity via Evolution

Parsons was a liberal, not a conservative (Alexander 2001). He could not accept in good conscience a societal community that integrates only the minority core group and justifies the exclusion and repression of those remaining outside. Yet, this is precisely the situation he conceptualized. How can he escape from such a dilemma? He might have theorized the contradictions. Could societal community be conceptualized so as to explain how and why integration in one part of society produces exclusion in others? Taking this path would involve critically examining "actually existing" forms of societal community, and would have challenged Parsons' affirmative attitude toward social integration. It would also have undermined his increasingly celebratory treatment of contemporary American society.

If Parsons had confronted the ambiguity of his societal community concept, he would have had to enter into the thicket of contradictions it entailed, exploring why and how actually existing societal communities become imbedded in, and disimbedded from, the values and powers of core groups. Rather than exploring ambiguity, Parsons engages in a kind of splitting. He makes use of evolutionary theory to place the "bad," nondemocratic societal community on one side of the evolutionary scale and the "good," democratic societal community on the other. Making his discussion linear rather than dialectical allows Parsons to emphasize progress and betterment over and against contradiction and tragedy.

The more democratic the societal community, the more congruence between integration, membership, and the entire territorial population. Parsons puts this possibility into evolutionary terms, making it a matter of moving from the traditional to the modern period. Among traditional forms of society, Parsons' favorite polemical targets are China and India. In Imperial China, despite the possibilities for integration opened up by social structure and culture, "the Confucian cultural system . . . prevented Imperial China from . . . including the masses of the population in the reorganized system" (Parsons 1966a: 77). As for India, "the duality which was central to its religious legitimation was never transcended in the direction of the inclusion of the nonprivileged in a more equalized societal community" (ibid.: 78–9).

The implication of these comparisons is that the exclusionary face of societal communities was confined to "earlier" and

70

non-Western societies. Insofar as modernity is achieved, Parsons believes, the tension between integration and justice will be resolved. "Contemporary social structure" he writes (1973: 99) with evident relief, "is characterized by a special kind of integration." What has happened is that subsystems which fused and overlapped in traditional society have "undergone a series of 'declarations of independence'" (ibid.). Just as the market, the state, and the family have become independent of one another, so has the societal community. It is no longer connected to core groups or to any particular value, but has become an abstract community of equals, "a single societal community with full citizenship for all" (Parsons 1966b: 740).

This more differentiated societal community – based on transcendental solidarity – was anticipated and precipitated by the evolutionary breakthroughs of world history. The possibility began with Greek philosophy, which Parsons calls "the first formal and general conceptualization of the normative framework of human life which clearly abstracted moral obligations" (1966a: 106). This early "breakthrough" was carried further by the European Renaissance and Reformation. These cultural highpoints contributed singularly to the process Parsons conceptualizes as "value generalization," the gradual separation of the culture that regulated society from the normative values of the core group. More institutional changes point in the same direction, involving an ongoing process of "structural differentiation." Taken together, value generalization and structural differentiation create "adaptive upgrading," the optimistic, ameliorating concept that Parsons employs to characterize historical development as such. With his evolutionary turn, Parsons compels integration to take a less primordial, less core-group centered form.

> Adaptive upgrading . . . *requires* that specialized functional capacities be freed from ascription within more diffuse structural units . . . Upgrading processes may *require* the inclusion in a status of full membership in the relevant general community system of previously excluded groups which have developed legitimate capacities to "contribute" to the functioning of the system. (1966a: 22, emphasis added)

The difficulty of maintaining such a buoyant outlook in the latter half of one of history's bloodiest centuries is not to be underestimated. One coping strategy is to avoid spending too much time on repressive and violent episodes that marred modernity's path. While Parsons expansively lauds the emancipatory achievements of the Reformation and Renaissance, his discussion of the more authoritarian and repressive Counter-Reformation is terse and condensed (see Alexander 1988c). As for the Nazi movement, "even with its immense mobilization of power," Parsons feels safe in concluding – with the 20/20 vision of hindsight – it "seems to have been an acute sociopolitical failure, but not a source of major future structural patterns" (1973: 130). Parsons even finds a way to be optimistic about the uncomfortable link between modernity and war. While acknowledging that "certainly the history of modern societal systems has been one of frequent, if not continuous, warfare," Parsons observes that "the *same* system of societies within which the evolutionary process that we have traced has occurred has been subject to a high incidence of violence, most conspicuously in war but also internally, including revolutions" (ibid.: 141, emphasis in original).[3] Why this observation is presented as reassuring is hard to say.

Parsons' major strategy for maintaining evolutionary optimism is to focus on the United States, which he calls "the new lead society" of contemporary modernity (1973: 86). For it is in the United States that:

> The principle of equality has broken through to a new level of pervasiveness and generality. A societal community as *basically* composed of equals seems to be the "end of the line" in the long process of undermining the legitimacy of . . . older, more particularistic ascriptive bases of membership. (ibid.: 118–19, emphasis in original)

With the emergence of American society, and especially its "maturation" during the civil rights era, Parsons believes that the conflict between integration and justice has disappeared. In terms of social evolution, it is the end of the line, or at least the beginning of the end.[4] The jealous god of evolution has been appeased.

Or has it? Despite his declarations that evolution is progressive and that the American societal community has fully evolved, Parsons cannot entirely avoid certain uncomfortable social facts. Repression and exclusion continue in contemporary societal communities, even the one in the United States. Rather than explaining why, however, Parsons makes a series of lexical exceptions to his semantic evolutionary rule. The presence of the pathologies afflicting modern societal communities is noted by conjunctive and adverbial qualifiers designed to demonstrate their absence. Parsons' evolutionary treatment of contemporary societies is punctuated by a grammar filled with buts, despites, howevers, of courses, and althoughs. It is through this grammatical technique that the particularistic repressions restricting actually existing societal communities are magically overcome.

> At one extreme, the principal content of the normative order may be considered more or less universal to all men. *However*, this raises acute problems of how far such high universalistic norms can be effectively institutionalized in the actual operations of so extensive a community ... [Thus,] modern societal communities have generally taken a form based upon nationalism. (ibid.: 20, emphasis added)

> In fully modern societies ... there can be diversity on each basis, religious, ethnic, and territorial, because the common status of citizenship provides a sufficient foundation for national solidarity ... The institutions of citizenship and nationality can *nevertheless* render the societal community vulnerable if the bases of pluralism are exacerbated into sharply structured cleavages. Since the typical modern community unifies a large population over a large territory, for example, its solidarity may be severely strained ... This is particularly true where ... regional cleavages coincided with ethnic and/or religious divisions. Many modern societies have disintegrated before varying combinations of these bases of cleavage. (ibid.: 22, emphasis added)

> *Despite* Ireland, therefore, Britain became relatively united ethnically. (ibid., emphasis added)

> American territory was *initially* settled *mainly* by one distinctive group of migrants ... The United States was *for a long time* an Anglo-Saxon society, which tolerated and granted legal rights to members of some other ethnic groups but did not fully include them. (ibid.: 87–8, emphasis added)

> Negroes are still in the early stages of the inclusion process ... It may, *however*, be predicted with considerable confidence that the *long-run* trend is toward successful inclusion. (ibid.: 89, emphasis added)

> *Although* American society has always been differentiated internally by class, it has never suffered the aftermath of aristocracy and serfdom that persisted so long in Europe. (ibid.: 90, emphasis added)

The participation of the wealthier and more educated groups . . . has been disproportionate, *but* there has also been a persistent populist strain and relative upward mobility. (ibid., emphasis added)

Although the franchise was originally restricted, especially by property qualifications, it was extended rapidly, and universal manhood suffrage, *except* for Negroes, was attained relatively early. (ibid.: 91, emphasis added)

On the whole, the structural outline of "citizenship" in the new societal community is complete *though not yet* fully institutionalized. (ibid.: 93 emphasis added)

This movement has thus meant an immense extension of equality of opportunity . . . At the same time, *however*, the educational system is necessarily selective. (ibid.: 95 emphasis added)

Although "discrimination" by lineage membership, social class, ethnic origin, religion, race, and so on is tenacious . . . (ibid.: 110, emphasis added)

In our general paradigm of social change, we have stressed the connection between inclusion and adaptive upgrading . . . *but* they are not identical. (1973: 115, emphasis added)

There are, *of course*, important flaws. One surely is war. (ibid.: 115, emphasis added)

The second mode is focused in the institutionalization of equality of opportunity . . . This ideal is *of course* very far from full realization. (ibid.: 120, emphasis added)

There has, *of course*, been a great deal of conflict, "frontier" primitivism, and lag in some of the older parts of the systems relative to the more progressive parts. (ibid.: 140, emphasis added)

Certainly the history of modern societal systems had been one of frequent, if not continual, warfare. (ibid., emphasis added)

The Ideological Moment and American Hubris

During the Cold War, Parsons wished to defend capitalist democracies against communist dictatorships, and for him such a defense entailed reading modernity in an "American" manner. It was as he moved from a more critical to a more complacent liberalism in these later writings that Parsons developed the concept of societal community. During the intense polarization of the late sixties, Parsons (1973: 116) did acknowledge that, despite his optimistic declarations about evolution, there was a "general moral malaise in modern society." He even went so far as to admit that "current widespread fears of imminent and ultimate nuclear holocaust raise a question that cannot be answered objectively with much confidence" (ibid.: 141). Rather than offer a systematic explanation for such fears and dangers, however, Parsons blames the messenger. Like many anti-radical theorists before him (e.g., Aron 1957), he accuses intellectuals of overlooking everything positive about modern life. "Contrary to the opinion among many intellectuals," he insists, "American society – and most modern societies without dictatorial regimes – has institutionalized a far broader range of freedoms than . . . any previous society" (ibid.: 114). The problem is not in modern society, but in the intellectuals who criticize it: "Ideological complexes with paranoid themes are very old indeed" (ibid.: 116). Parsons' ambition "is to establish sufficient doubt of the validity of such views" (ibid.: 141).

The Dialectics of Modernity

At one point, Parsons acknowledges that, while "in our general paradigm of social change we have stressed the connection between inclusion and adaptive upgrading[,] they are not identical" (ibid.: 115). This is an extraordinary admission. That they are identical was the point of Parsons' later, evolutionary theory. Still, Parsons does not try to explain, except in an occasional, ad hoc, and residual manner, what might constitute the gap in between. What might a more systematic effort at theoretical explanation entail?

To reconstruct a more satisfactory theory of the societal community, one would have to look closely at how processes of "anti-universalism" have often led to destruction rather than progress and how such negative processes are built into the core of modernity itself. One would need to ask: How has the modern societal community remained fused with market, state, and particularistic cultural communities, including those defined by class, race, sex, ethnicity, religion? (see chapter 7, below). How has such fusion allowed hierarchy and fragmentation to be legitimated in democratic societies? The gap between membership categories and populations-in-territory remains wide, and core group integration often proceeds at the expense of justice for stigmatized groups outside the centers of modern societies.[5]

If the endemic persistence of particularism and exclusion is so theorized, then one can dispense with the utopian idea that value consensus produces social integration, much less justice. The "index of incomplete institutionalization," Parsons (1973: 103) once suggested, "is the insistence by individuals and groups on recognition of their particular and partial 'rights' by means of techniques ranging from simple assertion to organized protest to obstruction." Parsons is suggesting that protests for rights expansion reflect the failure of modernity to become complete. It seems preferable to view rights-oriented conflict as evidence of the fullness of modernity, not of its failure but of its success. As Eisenstadt (Alexander 1992b) suggests in his quite different approach to value institutionalization, the tension between ideal and reality can never be eliminated (see chapter 3, above). The gulf initiated during the Axial Age will not be overcome; duality will always mark the modern and postmodern condition.[6]

By understanding the contradictions in Parsons' approach to societal community, one can envision what a more critical, dynamic, and systematic theory might be. There is, indeed, a sphere of solidarity that needs to be differentiated from other spheres if justice is to be achieved. In terms of its idealizing aspirations, such a "civil" sphere envisions a system of culture and institutions that rests upon demanding, universalistic norms of mutual respect, equality, and autonomy. The degree to which such a differentiated community actually exists can be empirically investigated and theoretically conceived. Such an investigation will demonstrate that the modern culture of rationality and universalism creates a shadow discourse of repression, and that the continuous fragmentation of actually existing civil spheres justifies core group domination and subjugation – even as it provides cultural leverage for institutions that pursue justice in turn.

Such an inquiry would expose new kinds of boundary relations, between the civil and uncivil spheres, and develop a theory, not only of facilitating inputs, but of destructive intrusions that trigger social movements for repair. This alternative approach to civic solidarity could explore the dark side of modernity, providing better theoretical resources for understanding the possibilities for civil repair.

― 5 ―

DESPISING OTHERS:
SIMMEL'S STRANGER

This chapter will criticize and deepen Georg Simmel's theory of the stranger, developing a cultural-sociological model of how modern civil spheres systematically pollute non-members. We begin with a news story from almost two decades ago about the treatment of darker skinned immigrants in France:

> Guy André Janvitary, a 32-year-old construction worker, left his apartment at 2 p.m. one recent day to look for jobs. By the time he returned early that evening, he had been stopped six times on the streets and strip-searched once by police. Why did authorities single out this law-abiding French citizen for scrutiny? There's only one reason: Janvitary has dark skin. And these days in France, people with dark skin are suspected of being Islamic fundamentalists and, hence, possible terrorists ... With no apologies, the police are focusing on dark-skinned people. And the random checks, sharply criticized by human rights groups, reflect a deeper French antipathy toward Muslims who insist on maintaining their cultural and theological traditions rather than assimilating French values and culture. "When the police see me, they just see a dark-skinned man, not a Frenchman," said Janvitary, who was born in Martinique and who has been "controlled," as the police call it, dozens of times in recent weeks. (Kraft 1994)

Before rethinking the "stranger" (Simmel 1950: 402–7), we must first acknowledge the originality of Simmel's concept vis-à-vis other, seemingly comparable ideas from the classical sociological tradition. The stranger is very different from the economically disadvantaged or exploited class, the theoretical category for those impoverished by an impersonal economic order and its elite that

Marx took to be the paradigmatic asymmetrical relationship of capitalist society. It is this theoretical category upon which contemporary studies of stratification have continued to concentrate up until today, even if they have defined class more by market position than productive mode. Nor can the stranger be seen as synonymous with the dominated, administratively subordinated, politically disenfranchised status Weber explored in his theory of authority. Simmel's category also differs fundamentally from the idea of the egoist, the anomic, and the criminal, by which Durkheim represented inversions of solidarity in the structural theory of his early and middle years. Finally, the stranger is not the deviant of classical functionalist theory (e.g., Best 2004) that Parsons described before he developed the more promising, if ideologically compromised theory of societal inclusion in his later years.

The "Stranger" and Other Classical Tropes

What makes Simmel's theory fundamentally different from these others? In the first place, he is talking about a categorically constructed otherness – "constructed" in the contemporary cultural and cognitive sense (e.g., Seidman 2003) – rather than about some natural condition. Despite the reservations I will express below, it is important to note how vital the phenomenological and hermeneutical dimension is to Simmel's idea of what the stranger is about. Simmel insists that the stranger is understood and experienced as in, but not entirely of, his society. This distinguishes the stranger from other classical categories; Simmel seeks more subtle degrees of differentiation and discrimination. The stranger is not experienced by the host society simply as lower or excluded; rather, she is sensed to be different in some more fundamental way, even as she remains in some important sense a member of the wider society itself. With the stranger, then, Simmel's idea of negation becomes more closely connected with postmodern understandings of otherness (e.g., Seidman 2013). Because it is more cultural and more complex than the negative categories of other classical work, it is more useful for us to think with today. It also tells us more about the society in which we live.

If Simmel discovered this new and fundamentally important social category, however, he was not entirely successful either in defining its qualities or isolating its causes. After revisiting Simmel's original essay, and raising theoretical questions about it, I will look at some empirical examples of strangeness as they have been interpreted by contemporary humanities and social science scholars. I will then turn to Lewis Coser's "The Stranger in the Academy," an effort to apply Simmel's model to Simmel himself that appeared half a century ago (Coser 1965). In order to throw more light on the limitations of Simmel's early exemplar, I will examine its capacity to explain the unnerving historical document that Coser first revealed: the virulently anti-Semitic evaluation of Simmel made by one Dietrich Schaefer, an outside expert to whom the Baden *Kulturministerium* turned in 1908 when considering Simmel for a chair in philosophy at Heidelberg.

The Problem of Social Reduction

Today we all "know" what the concept "stranger" suggests, and common sense knowledge was no doubt just as perspicacious during the period when Simmel himself wrote. Weber, however, famously warned us against taking the common sense understanding of actors as our own. Simmel himself relied on common social understanding when he formulated his model, and one could argue he relied on it too much.

The paradox of Simmel's model is that, despite his subtle framing of strangeness, he spends very little time exploring the *meaning* of "stranger" in contemporary German or more broadly Western European culture. He does not undertake a hermeneutic investigation of what Dilthey called the *Objectif Geist*, or what we today would call "cultural structures" (Alexander 2003b) – the codes, narratives, and tropes that create the background understandings from which an idea like strangeness emerges and within which it continues to be reproduced.

Simmel (1950: 403) comes close to such an interpretive approach in his linguistic aside, early in the essay, to the effect that the stranger "is no 'owner of soil'," adding that he means "soil not only in the physical, but also in the figurative sense of a life substance which is fixed, if not in a point in space, at least in an ideal point of the social environment." This aside is revealing. As I will suggest below, it is not an objective position in physical or social space but an interpretive position vis-à-vis the "social ideal" that is the critical factor in creating the stranger in society.

Yet, Simmel does not develop the kind of culturally mediated approach this illuminating reference to the figurative suggests. Instead, he confines himself to the restrictive task that occupies so much of his formal sociology. Exploring the stranger as a social status produced by so-called structural forces, he focuses almost exclusively on determinate forces of a spatial and ecological kind. The stranger, Simmel (1950: 404) writes, results from "a particular structure composed of distance and nearness." Vis-à-vis the host society, the status of stranger is determined by the intersection of two physical positions – "the liberation from every given point in space" and the "fixation at such a point" (Simmel 1950: 402). Simmel elaborates this spatial paradox in a language that suggests the subjective ambiguity the position itself creates. Distance means that "he, who is close by, is far, and strangeness means that he, who also is far, is actually near" (ibid.). Simmel insists that the stranger's identity inside his own particular group is determined in a similarly objectified way: "He is fixed within a particular spatial group, or within a group *whose boundaries are similar to spatial boundaries*" (ibid., emphasis added). For Simmel, in other words, it is a social structural status in the quasi-physical sense that determines the orientation adopted by members of the host society.

How do these external, objective exigencies lead to strangeness? They force members of the host society to assume toward the outsider an abstract, generalizing point of view: "The proportion of nearness [or] remoteness," writes Simmel (1950: 406), in a manner that emphasizes his sense of the materiality he imputes to cause, "finds practical expression in the more abstract nature of the relation to him." The distinctive spatial connection produces a distinctive subjective orientation, one that contrasts with other spatial connections and the orientations they produce: "With the stranger one has only certain more general qualities in common, whereas the relation to more organically connected persons is

81

based on the commonness of specific differences from merely general features" (ibid.). The causal sequence goes from social structure to subjective abstraction to negative emotional feelings: "Because the common features are general, they add . . . an element of coolness" (ibid.).

What exactly does Simmel mean when he associates stranger status with generality and commonality, rather than with specificity and difference? By emphasizing nearness, Simmel insists that the stranger is not entirely a distant object. Evidently, he believes that some basic sense of connection is established with the host group because the stranger is not only far but also near. The occupant of this status, he emphasizes, is also involved in "very positive social relation[s]" with the host society, e.g. the merchant who mediates between foreign markets and domestic trade. Nearness is also important for Simmel's rhetorical interests, for it allows him to be ironical in his precociously postmodern way. He (1950: 402) goes so far as to suggest, indeed, that being a stranger "is a specific form of interaction" that is "an element of the group itself." Nonetheless, Simmel believes such functionally important activities remain marginalized. The host group's orientations are generalized and abstract, and hence cool in their tone.

While such theoretical reasoning is consistent with the Romantic notion of expressive individualism within which Simmel worked, one is entitled to ask why generality and abstraction necessarily imply negative judgment and feelings. Why does the physical position of being near yet far seem strange rather than ominous, frightening, or mysteriously attractive? The answer is that, for Simmel, genuine feelings of warmth and attachment can be formed only if there exists a concrete rather than abstract relation between the knower and the known, only, that is, if one views the other as a unique rather than representative human being. Concrete ties cannot be produced with one who is "also far." In their absence, even if abstraction and generality produce ideas about common humanity, feelings of real connectedness cannot be formed. Thus, "the stranger is close to us," Simmel regretfully observes, only "insofar as we feel between him and ourselves *common* features of a national, social, occupational, or generally human, nature" (1950: 406, emphasis added).

But if such notions of common humanity do exist, might they not actually be grounds for acceptance rather than for strangeness? Simmel disagrees, because he assumes an intrinsic connection between abstraction and alienation. The "extraordinary and basic preponderance" of common orientations "over the *individual* elements that are exclusive with [a] particular relationship," he writes (ibid., emphasis added), prevents any real knowledge: "He is far from us, insofar as these common features extend beyond him or us, and connect us only because they connect a great many people" (ibid.).

The Indeterminate Relation of Structure and Orientation

I now take issue with Simmel's emphasis on the structural status of strangeness, which implies that the meaning of strangeness reflects spatial position and behavioral relation. I suggest, instead, that to understand strangeness we must focus on the cultural interpretation of social structures and the categories within which these active interventions are made.[1] When we do so, we will see that it is the construction of difference, not commonality, that makes potentially marginal groups into dangerous ones that are strange.

To be sure, one can think of many groups who seem to be the strangers Simmel describes. Jewish bankers in medieval France performed functions that others either could not or would not do; they were never full citizens, but they were often protected subjects of the king. Middle-class black Americans, who lived in the northern United States before World War I, served whites in roles like barber and tailor, were well respected professionally, and lived in integrated residential settings. Chinese, Korean, and Southeast Asian immigrants in California have worked in "middle-men" positions for more than a century, as did southern European immigrants in the American Midwest and the Irish in the Northeast. Indian and Chinese immigrants formed the merchant class in various parts of Africa. When German and Austrian Jews streamed into the US during the late 1930s, many worked as writers, editors, translators, psychoanalysts, and scientists.

These illustrations, however, raise doubts, both about Simmel's structural approach and the evaluative tone this status is supposed to imply. It would seem that virtually every excluded group has, at some point in its career, performed economic or political roles that could be interpreted as placing them in but not of their societies. This very universality makes for questionable explanatory value. On the one hand, members of groups never convicted of strangeness, such as Protestant English immigrants to Massachusetts Bay Colony in the first half of the seventeenth century, were forced to undergo years of indentured servitude before they were allowed to assume positions as equal workers and citizens. Structural marginality, in other words, need not be accompanied by strangeness. On the other hand, groups who were indelibly tabooed by otherness can be said to have played functionally indispensable roles. Would anyone argue, for example, that black slavery was not essential to the plantation economy of the US? Evidently, functional importance does not necessarily produce abstract feelings of commonality. When they worked as slaves, black Americans were despised, categorized by their white masters as closer to animals than to human beings. It was not commonality and abstractness that accompanied this functional importance, but a sense of extraordinary and fundamental difference, illustrated with concrete images of a racist kind. Today, even when many American blacks have achieved middle and working-class status, and interact occupationally with whites, they are rarely integrated either residentially or by marriage into the core of American society, and their common humanity still remains suspect to many Americans, if not a majority.

It is instructive to note the contrast with the experience of many immigrants who fled Europe in the 1930s. As historical studies such as H. Stuart Hughes' *The Sea Change* (1975) indicate, and personal memoirs such as Lewis Coser's (1993) also attest, these immigrants' initial marginality was often rather quickly converted into high status positions. Despite inevitable discomforts, the horrifying backdrop of war and persecution to which Jewish Europeans were subject created a common bond between these strangers and their American host communities that was pronounced and profound. Americans who never encountered these immigrants as concrete human beings experienced a symbolic identification that stimulated feelings of generosity, warmth, and concern. These were not the only reactions, of course. Nativistic xenophobia about "100 per cent Americanism" remained, and became stronger soon after the war. Nonetheless, this case, as well as the others I have mentioned, suggests that the strict relationship between structural position, cultural abstraction, and emotional hostility cannot be maintained.

The Importance of Symbolic Action

The alternative I have in mind is straightforward. It is a question of the relative autonomy of culture. Feelings of strangeness towards others are produced by the active employment of distinctive standards of interpretation. These standards are constructed from polarized, dichotomous symbolic structures that draw from a centuries old discourse (Alexander and Smith 1993, 2003) about what kinds of persons are in and out, about the qualities and feelings that are deserving of honor and liberty versus those that, calling out pollution, need to be repressed. The objects of the negative, polluting side of this discourse are often functional intermediaries or outgroups, rarely those in the highest stratum of society. But vis-à-vis many groups of intermediate status, the truly denigrating forms of civil discourse are not applied, whereas vis-à-vis other groups of much higher status they are indeed. It is not structural position per se, but rather its active interpretation and reconstruction in terms of polluted representations, that leads the occupants of this status to assume a strangeness in the core group's eyes. Once they are so labeled and delegitimated, their social position is often altered to be more congruent with their cultural status.[2]

As Massey and Denton (1993) documented, the physical segregation of American blacks did not precede white people's cultural construction of their strangeness. To the contrary, for decades before World War I, African Americans lived amidst white populations and often worked among them and with them as well. However, because Northern whites shared the national core group's racist culture, faced with the massive postwar black immigration they took away this opportunity to live among whites in a dispersed and heterogeneous way. Blacks became strictly segregated, and what became known as the ghetto was born. Deeply entrenched feelings of strangeness toward black people had inspired political and economic actions, which in turn created separate ecological positions, a separation that prevented economic mobility and reinforced the culture of racism.

If we are really to understand what makes the stranger, we must look more closely at the role that such an active intervention of culture plays. When we do, we observe something which, while at first glance tautological, actually opens our investigation of strangeness to causal processes of a new kind. We discover that the employment of the *language* of strangeness creates the strangeness of a status, not the other way around. This is not to deny that many and various social structural pressures come into play. Imperialism may lead to the demand for rationalizing ideology; immigration may lead to the need to defend jobs; economic impoverishment may lead to renewed class conflict; military defeat or political instability may provide opportunities for new social actors to take power. None of these factors, however, can, in and of themselves, specify who will be constructed as strange, or how.

Not only the objective but the subjective status of core groups (Alexander 1988b) must be challenged for strangeness to be assigned; only then, if fear becomes subjective, will polarizing categories apply. Core groups do not feel frightened by every entering or potentially marginal group. Do they share race, religion, language, or ethnic origin? If these primordial qualities overlap significantly with the core group's own, the hosts will be more inclined to believe that the newcomers are not actually strange after all. As a result, they will not need to defend themselves by drawing upon the categories of pollution that members of civil society always find close at hand.

Insofar as such purportedly primordial qualities do not overlap, and certainly there is no exact structural calculus for predicting when they feel like they do and do not, these distantiating categories come more decisively into play. The possibility of strangeness now becomes the palpable certainty of it; fear of outsiders now seems to be based on reality. The decisive factor is cultural action. Groups are *made* strange by the active intervention of interpreting subjects. Challenged by objective possibilities and frightened by subjective threats, intellectuals, political leaders, and ordinary persons alike move to create a division between "us" and "them."[3] They desire to create boundaries, to be separated from these others. But, contrary to the more middle-period Durkheimianism of Kai Erikson (1966) or Mary Douglas and Aaron Wildavsky (1982), those who create social divisions are not preserving community simply for community's sake, much less for some status interest, if that term is interpreted in an instrumental sense. Core groups act to create social boundaries that are "always already" there (Lamont 2000). Drawing upon long-standing symbolic structures, they experience certain groups as strange and frightening. It is to protect themselves against those who have been so constructed that they draw the wagons around.

Forms of Strangeness and the Discourse of Repression

Let me illustrate this revision of Simmel's structural perspective with some empirical examples of how interpretive categories about strangeness come into play.[4]

Colonial Domination

On the first page of Edward Said's *Orientalism*, he reminds us of precisely the general theoretical point I have been trying to make. "The Orient," he writes (1978: 1), "is not only adjacent to Europe" physically, but it is "its cultural contestant, and one of its deepest and most recurring images of the Other." Despite its physical proximity and the frequency of commercial interaction, "the Orient is not an inert fact of nature," Said insists; "it is not merely *there*" (1978: 4, emphasis in original).

> Men make their own history . . . and extend it to geography . . . The Orient is an idea that has a history and a tradition of thought, imagery, and vocabulary that has given it reality and presence in and for the West. (1978: 5)

When we look at the reconstruction Said makes of orientalist ideas themselves – a hermeneutical excursion that illuminates a culture structure extending over four centuries – we see the familiar polarities between reason and irrationality, autonomy and dependence, honor and self-interest, conscience and greed, equality and hierarchy that have been used time and again to establish the strangeness of those who are unfit to enter into civil society. One small example must suffice. Between 1882, when Britain first occupied Egypt and put an end to the nationalist rebellion of Colonel Arbi, and 1907, Britain's colonial administrator was Evelyn Baring. After his retirement, this former official, now the honorable Lord Cromer, published his thoughts about who his former subjects really were and why they had merited the repression of British rule.[5] Whereas Westerners are "conscientious" and motivated by "unselfish conduct," Lord Cromer wrote, he had found the Oriental to be "devoid of energy and initiative" and "lethargic and suspicious." It is self-evident, according to Lord Cromer, that the European is a "close reasoner," "sceptical," bound by "truth," "principle," and a "cosmopolitan allegiance." By contrast, he found those whom the European was colonizing to be exactly the opposite. For the Egyptian, "accuracy is abhorrent"; his mind "easily degenerates into untruthfulness"; it is "wanting in lucidity" and "symmetry" and is constricted by "narrow nationalism." Is it any wonder that these "subject races" need to be colonized, and that the colonizer must make every effort, through both force and persuasion, to create "a stronger bond of union between the rulers and the ruled"?

Racial Domination

If any group in America can be seen as a structurally produced "stranger" community, it would be members of the black underclass, not only economically degraded by generations of poverty, but physically separated from whites in different economic classes. The streets of the transitional neighborhoods that border America's urban ghettos are viewed by many social scientists, in fact, as paradigmatic arenas for the interplay of structural forces.

City streets seem like merely physical spaces framing impersonal interactions, an objectification underlined by the racial and class structuring of underclass life. In his ethnographic study of public behavior in such transitional neighborhoods, Elijah Anderson challenges this perspective. His findings vividly demonstrate how categories of meaning create strangeness even in the most objectively degraded arenas of human life.

Much as Said opened his work, Anderson begins his pivotal chapter, "Street Etiquette and Street Wisdom," by attacking the notion that space has a merely physical status. Evoking such a determinist perspective, he takes a hypothetical look at the streets in "Village," the transitional town that borders the underclass ghetto, "Norton."

> Usually pedestrians can walk there undisturbed. Often they seem peaceful. Always they have an elegant air, with mature trees, wrought-iron fences, and solid architecture reminiscent of prewar comfort and ease. (Anderson 1990: 207)

However, this physical appearance, and these behavioral facts, are not reflected in the subjective understandings of Village inhabitants themselves. "In the minds of current residents," Anderson discovered, "the streets are dangerous and volatile" (ibid.). When the middle-class white residents of Village walk their streets, they encounter strangers of whom they are afraid. In part, Anderson acknowledges, this fear is based on objective experience with reality:

> Muggings occur with some regularity. Cars are broken into for tape decks and other valuables. Occasionally people suffer seemingly meaningless verbal or even physical assaults. (ibid.)

For these objective reasons, Village residents "know they should distrust" (ibid.) some of the people they meet in the streets. At the same time, Anderson insists, such distrust does not emerge automatically, as a reflection of actual experiences, impersonal social forces, or physical space. To the contrary, he suggests, developing distrust "requires tremendous energy" (ibid.). When it is achieved, moreover, it goes way beyond actual experiences to cover whole categories of people.

Anderson closely studied the fleeting public interactions that occurred between middle-class whites and ghetto blacks, the "few crucial seconds [in which] people are conditioned to rapid scrutiny of the looks, speech, public behavior, gender, and color of those sharing the environment" (1990: 208). Finding interpretive action everywhere at work, he focused on the cultural categories within which they were framed. "Public awareness is color-coded," Anderson observes (ibid.):

> Simplistic racial interpretation . . . creates a "we/they" dichotomy between whites and blacks . . . White skin denotes civility, law-abiding-ness, and trustworthiness, while black skin is strongly associated with poverty, crime, incivility, and distrust. (ibid.)

The codes regulating street life connect color and class to the discursive categories of civil society, to self-control versus the lack of it, to respect for others versus aggression, to the ability to be rational (which creates trust) and vice versa. These categories are not merely cognitive; their negative sides are morally and emotion-ally polluting. The people to whom they apply must be kept at bay. Anderson (1990: 216) shows that "the collective definitions of 'safe', 'harmless', 'trustworthy', 'bad', 'dangerous', and 'hostile' become part of the Village perspective." He documents how "reports of personal experiences, including 'close calls' and 'horror stories', initiate and affirm neighborhood communion." It is a subjective "perspective," he insists, not the objective fact of spatial position itself, that "creates social distance." The end result, of course, looks deceptively the same. Living in but not of white society, young black men are strangers inspiring decidedly cool emotions in the whites they meet. An unknown young black male is readily deferred to. If he asks for anything, his request must be handled quickly and summarily. If he is persistent, help must be summoned (Anderson 1990: 208).

Class Domination

Not only races and civilizations, but rival social classes and nations have been interpreted as strangers to each other for the same reasons and with similar effects. Since the early days of industrial capitalism, for example, conservatives have tried to legitimate efforts to block egalitarian social movements by generating public alarm about "the Red scare." They have done so by making efforts to link manual workers, socialist and communist leaders, radical intellectuals and students, and middle-class muckrakers to the same polluted categories that Said and Anderson evoke. The 1848 revolutionary uprising in France, for example, increased the size of the electorate from a quarter million to more than 10 million, of whom three-quarters were peasants and a good third illiterate. While "republicans" dominated the Provisional Government, self-proclaimed socialists were represented as well. A massive backlash against the new government's reforms emerged, and harsh repression followed the subsequent victory of the right. While these dramatic moves were highly polarizing, they gained significant public support, so much so that a long period of relative stability followed under the rule of Napoleon III. One reason for the right's success in countering the leftward surge was its success in categorizing the democratic forces as enemies of civilization. The familiar negative categories are strikingly employed, for example, in the call to arms issued by a rightist named Henri Wallon, in May 1849:

> A red is not a man, he is a red. . . . He is not a moral, intelligent, and free being like you or me . . . He is a fallen and degenerate man. His face is marked by signs of that fall. A beaten appearance, brutalized . . . eyes as colorless as those of a pig . . . the mouth as mute and senseless as that of an ass . . . The "dividers" have written on their faces the stupidity of the doctrines and ideas by which they live. (quoted in Goubert 1988: 248)

National Conflict

Relations among nations have been distorted in similar ways. Richard Kuisel has documented the extraordinarily stable set of categories that have mediated French perceptions of the United States. The emergence of America as a major industrial nation during the interwar years stimulated many influential French intellectuals to formulate their "national identity . . . through negation, by establishing a counter-identity, by constructing a 'we'/'them' dichotomy" (Kuisel 1993: 6).[6]

Compared to the putative maturity of the French, for example, Americans were defined as *les grands enfants* (big children) who represented the "new barbarism." In contrast with French *civilisation* and its emphasis on *honneur*, Americans were portrayed as "ignorant manipulators," or as "comfortable brutes" who resembled animals more than humans. "What strikes the European traveler" in America, the French writer Duhamel observed in 1931, "is the progressive approximation of human life to what we know of the way of life of insects." As such, Americans were not believed to possess the qualities necessary for democratic society. Duhamel notes, for example, "the same effacement of the individual, the same progressive reduction and unification of social types . . . the same submission of every one to those obscure exigencies of the hive or of the anthill." At the same time, American civilization, or the lack of it, was likened to a machine. The "box-like skyscrapers," the "over-sized cities," the thirst for material goods – all these had made America into a "technicized horror of inhuman efficiency."

Americans were being *made* strange to the French. In the early years of the twentieth century, this strangeness "explained" how Americans could be so dominated by capitalism; in the eyes of both the radical French left and the religious French right, Americans were merely "happy slaves." In mid-century, the same categories were employed to warn against the imminent "American conquest" of France. Because Americans had so often been *conceived* as deprived of the rational and human qualities necessary for civil life, it was difficult for postwar French people to welcome American soldiers, administrators, businessmen, and intellectuals as either liberators, much less as guides. The postwar American represented an authoritarian threat to the French way of life. Americans were "occupiers" (Duhamel 1931: 32), and they would have to be ejected. Only in the late 1960s, with the emergence of the new youth culture and fundamental changes in the social structure of France itself, did these categorical representations begin to change. America began to seem more capable of generating an active civic life, and Americans were more frequently seen as attractive rather than strange.

Was Simmel "Strange"?: Anti-Semitism Versus Sociology

In 1908 Simmel was considered for a Chair in Philosophy at Heidelberg University. His failure to win the position can be linked, in part at least, to the influence of anti-Semitism at the highest levels of German university life. This is well illustrated in the 1908 letter of evaluation provided by Dietrich Schaefer. Schaefer concentrated on the unconventional elements in Simmel's academic profile, particularly on the enormously popular public lectures he gave in Berlin, from which many of his published essays emerged. Constructing the man, the lectures, and the audience in the familiar patterns of civil and anti-civil dichotomies, Schaefer demonstrated that Simmel was a stranger in the German university system and did not deserve inclusion at the highest levels of the nation's academic life.

Fifty years later, in an article published in the *American Journal of Sociology* (1958), Lewis Coser looked back at this historical incident. While acknowledging Simmel's intellectual unconventionality and the iconoclasm of his popular lecturing style, Coser suggested a sociological explanation for the attribution of strangeness, and he employed as his explanatory model Simmel's own theory. Coser suggested that the social structures that had impinged on Simmel had made it impossible for him to conform to the typical norms of German academic life. Without denying some empirical and theoretical grounding for Coser's explanation, I wish to suggest that this social structural argument does not go far enough. The interpretation of cultural structures is just as important for explaining Simmel's strangeness as social structures of a more material kind.

Indeed, if we look closely at Coser's own "social" explanation, we can see it as implicitly offering an interpretation of Simmel in cultural terms. The value-laden terms Coser employs to characterize Simmel project a purging antidote to the repressive moral discourse that Simmel's anti-Semitic critics applied. By emphasizing the effect of external social structures on Simmel, Coser can portray Simmel as a rational actor, not a strange one. If Simmel's unconventional behavior were a reasonable response to circumstances, it is implied, any other German academic would have behaved in the same way. Simmel was not strange, therefore, and his anti-Semitic critics were wrong to say so. He was capable of participating fully in German civil life.

Schaefer employed dichotomous moral codes to characterize both himself and Simmel. He began his confidential letter to the Baden *Kulturminister* by underlining his own openness and universalism, his determination to "express my opinion about Professor Simmel quite frankly."[7] Noting that Simmel was a "dyed-in-the-wool Israelite, in his outward appearance, in his bearing, and in his manner of thinking," Schaefer professes "it is not necessary to adduce this fact" to explain why Simmel had thus far been denied promotion. The reasons, rather, have to do with Simmel's actual qualities of mind. The qualities to which Schaefer points, however, turn out to bear striking similarities to anti-Semitic stereotypes about the Jewish mind.

Schaefer devotes the heart of his letter to explaining why Simmel's lectures show him to be intellectually unqualified, despite their being "well attended . . . well rounded, succinct, and polished." These lectures, Schaefer claims, actually offer "little material" of a scholarly kind. The scholarly deficit is camouflaged because Simmel "speaks exceedingly slowly, by dribs and drabs" and because "he spices his words with clever sayings." Simmel's lecture halls are filled to brimming because "these features are very much appreciated by certain categories of students." Schaefer proceeds to analogize the polluted categories of Simmel, Israelite thinker and superficial lecturer, with other kinds of persons and regions who are symbolically degraded in ways the readers of his letter will tacitly understand. He notes, for example, that "the ladies constitute a very large portion" of Simmel's audience. He observes that there is "an extraordinarily numerous contingent of the *oriental* world" who are "still flooding in semester after semester from the countries to the East." Simmel's "whole manner," Schaefer suggests, "is in tune with" the "orientation and taste" of these groups, who demand "titillating stimulation or volatile intellectual pleasure." Schaefer contaminates Simmel by metonymically associating him with sexual desires that civilized persons should normally repress.

These associations make it impossible for Simmel's intellectual qualities to be conceived in anything other than a negative way. Rather than "solid and systematic thinking," Simmel operates more by "bias" and "wit," even by "pseudo-wit." Rather than ideas that "lay foundations and build up," Simmel's "undermine and negate." Rather than being motivated by "scholarly zeal," Simmel is propelled by "a thirst for notoriety." In short, Simmel is strange. The "world view and philosophy of life which Simmel represents," Schaefer concludes, are "only too obviously different from our German Christian-classical education." This education, and Germany and Christianity more broadly, must be protected from pollution. Schaefer's conclusion follows logically from these analogical symbolic constructions: "There are more desirable . . . occupants for Heidelberg's second chair."

It is notable that Coser actually accepts some of the bare bones empirical phenomena that Schaefer had earlier described. He categorizes them, however, in sharply contrasting ways: "Simmel, the marginal man, the stranger, presented his academic peers not with a methodical and painstakingly elaborate system, but a series of often-disorderly insights, testifying to amazing powers of perception" (Coser 1965: 36–7). Following the social structural emphasis of Simmel himself, Coser points to an "external" basis for Simmel's unconventional style. Given his subordinate position in the German university and the opportunity structures available to him, Coser tells us, it should not seem surprising that Simmel offered lectures to the paying public rather than academic seminars, producing stylistic and intellectual essays rather than systematic philosophy as a result:

> While the popular teacher may incur the displeasure of peers, he may in exchange gain the approval of other role partners, his lecture public or audience. Do we not have here some warranty to assume that, hurt and rebuffed as he may have been by the lack of recognition within the academy, Simmel came to rely increasingly on the approval of his lecture audience and hence to accentuate in his written style as well as in his oral delivery those characteristics that brought applause? (Coser 1965: 34).

Yet, while Coser believes Simmel's choice was an eminently sensible one, he also believes it to have been "a major structural basis for the possible disturbance" of the "stable role-set" expected of German university scholars (Coser 1965: 33). The problem is that an audience, as compared to seminar students, "does not necessarily judge the lecturer in terms of his systematic and methodological gathering of evidence and his disciplined pursuit of painstaking research." Such a lecturer is judged, instead, by "the brilliance of his performance, the novelty of his ideas, and the ability to fascinate" (ibid.). By emphasizing social structure in this way, Coser is not only making an empirical-theoretical claim but challenging the stereotyped categories of degradation employed to justify Simmel's academic subordination. Employing the antonyms of these categories, he attaches Simmel to purifying qualities that deserve praise. Coser suggests not only that Simmel's desire to lecture was rational – a key evaluative term in discursive conflicts over strangeness – but that his lecturing style was neither self-indulgent nor ostentatious but conscientiousness. "All contemporary accounts" of his lecturing, Coser (1965: 33) writes, "agree that Simmel lived up to . . . audience expectations superlatively."

While ostensibly engaging in scientific explanation – one that eschews cultural for structural causality – Coser is actually constructing a moral counter-discourse that challenges the symbolic categories Schaefer employed to describe Simmel's audience. Rather than civilizational, racial, or gender signifiers, Coser references intellectual and cosmopolitan ones. Acknowledging that many of those attending Simmel's lectures were outsiders to professional sociology, he describes the origins of the audience in terms that stress its intelligence and dignity. Simmel's audiences were filled with students "from the most varied disciplines" and with "unattached intellectuals" from "the world of publishing, journalism, and the arts." It is true that a "goodly number of members of 'society'" also attended, but they did so because they were "in search of intellectual stimulation," not titillation. In other words, Coser describes Simmel's academic performances as anything but demonstrations of deviance and marginality. To the contrary, Simmel's lectures placed him at the center of public life of Wilhelmian Germany: "It is no exaggeration to say that many of Simmel's lectures were public events and often described as such in the newspapers" (Coser 1965: 33).

Once Coser has established not only the rationality of Simmel's motivation but the civil credentials of Simmel's audience, he employs these attributes to purify the polluting descriptions of the actual contents of Simmel's lectures, and to make a direct case for the brilliance and lucidity of Simmel himself. He does so by quoting from accounts offered by members of Simmel's audience (Coser 1965: 33–4). These testimonies emphasize, not Simmel's effort to titillate, but his intellectual "passion," which "was expressed not in words only, but also in gestures, movements, actions." The emotional and imagistic quality of his speaking represented brilliance, not a lack of substantial ideas: "His intensity of speech indicated a supreme tension of thought [which] sprang from lived concern." The palpable identification of Simmel's audience with his person resulted, not from nefarious seduction or elocutionary trick, but from the impression Simmel conveyed of a true intellectual at work.

The Ideological Affinities of Cultural and Structural Theory

Coser has employed Simmel's structural theory of the stranger to show that Simmel was not himself strange. In characterizing his argument, he quotes a remark that makes his cultural-cum-therapeutic ambition remarkably clear. Referencing the paradigmatic "structural" text of mid-century sociology, Robert Merton's *Social Theory and Social Structure*, Coser writes that "social structures generate the circumstances in which infringement of social codes constitutes a 'normal' (that is to say, an expectable) response" (Coser 1965: 30). Referring to objective social structures has the effect of normalizing actors. It allows them to be portrayed as rational, which is a particularly good tactic to employ in political debate. Political conservatives convict marginal groups of character flaws that make them seem responsible for their own fate. On the left of the political spectrum, by contrast, society itself is convicted, not the individual self. The left reserves its polluting rhetorical structures for social elites. The anticultural bias of contemporary "social structural" theory is perfectly fitted for

97

sociology's own left-leaning ideological task (e.g., Wilson 1987: 3–20).

My point in this chapter has been to suggest that such an external emphasis, while an ideological advantage, is a theoretical flaw. Strangeness is socially produced, and material circumstances are very much involved. But strangeness is always also produced in culturally-mediated ways that reference constructions of the subjective motivations of the actors themselves. It is this volitional component, these elements of deeply experienced emotion and profoundly convincing belief, that make strangeness so much more awful and demonic than Simmel allowed. Strangeness is produced by the conviction that the other is not fully human. This conviction makes it seem not only possible, but even necessary to exclude him, and such willed exclusion sometimes take on violent forms.

In an anomalous paragraph in his original essay, Simmel (1950: 407, emphasis added) acknowledges that "there *is* a kind of 'strangeness' that rejects the very commonness based on something more general which embraces the parties." The relation of the Greeks to the Barbarians is illustrative, as are other cases in which it is precisely general attributes, felt to be specifically and purely human, that are disallowed to the other. Simmel rejects, however, the broader theoretical relevance of this situation. This Greek conception of the stranger, he cautions, "has no positive meaning." The relation of the Barbarian to the Greek "is not what is relevant here" because the Barbarian is not "a member of the group itself." Yet, isn't this precisely the point? Strangers are, at one and the same time, group members and "non-relations." Those who survived the twentieth century understood this only too well.

— 6 —

MEANING EVIL

The social sciences have not given evil its due. Social evil has not been sufficiently respected; it has been deprived of intellectual attention. Evil is a powerful and sui generis social force. It deserves to be studied in a direct and systematic way.

Modernist Common Sense

This is not to suggest that the deficiencies of our societies – our "social problems" – have not been of great concern to social scientists. Nothing could be further from the truth. From its beginning, sociology in particular has been motivated by a reforming zeal for uplift and purification. Its practitioners, great and small, have conscientiously directed their studies to what they have taken to be the sources of social evil: oppression, domination, inequality, racism, sexism, xenophobia, and corruption.

What these studies have not demonstrated is theoretical reflexivity about what might be called the significance of evil as such. For social scientists have conducted their studies in the framework of common sense.[1] Within this framework, what is evil and what is good "go without saying." The orientation to good and evil is informed by an implicit assumption of objective transparency, of obviousness. Rather than problematizing the categorical distinctions themselves, the existence of the good and the evil is assumed to be natural, and social scientific effort is devoted, not to explaining how the categories came to be established, but to explaining how particular social manifestations of these categories come into being. Earlier social scientists asked: How is the "criminal mind" or the "sociopath" formed? What makes underdeveloped societies primitive? Later studies asked: How is crime created by poverty? Homophobia by prejudice or lack of education? Political extremism by endemic racism? How does globalization distort local economic development? In each of these cases, the dependent variable is taken as representing a social evil. The point has been to find the independent variable that explains it, not to question how it is that a highly negative evaluation for the dependent variable came into being.

The implication of the common sense approach to evil is that, when and if these social causes and effects are altered, social problems will be banished from the world and good will reign.[2] But what if evil can never be eliminated from the social world, no matter how well motivated or effective social reform? What if a principal point of sociology, and indeed the other ameliorating social sciences, is not to do away with evil but actually to establish the reality of its existence?[3]

This is not to suggest moral relativism or political resignation, but rather the necessity to make a fundamental break with the framework of modernist common sense.

The Cultural Turn and the Problem of Evil

To break from the path of common sense, we must follow a cultural turn that naturalistically minded social scientists resist. Perhaps good and evil should be seen, in the first instance, as products of cultural understanding, not as the results of social arrangements in and of themselves? Perhaps evil is an effect, an inevitable and necessary result, of the act of social interpretation, of the categorical system human beings employ to make sense of the societies in which they live?

It seems likely, in fact, that the objects of sociological investigations of evil are relative and historically various. There is less a naturalistic, objectively given conflict between good and evil

100

– between "positive" and "healthy" social forms, such as law, equality, or religion, and "negative" or "sick" forms, such as criminality, domination, or alienation – than a culturally constructed division whose substantive content is variable in the extreme. From this perspective, reformist social analysis is more, and less, than a scientific effort to sketch cause or even a hermeneutical effort to understand meaning. It is, in addition, a morally inspired symbolic effort to establish the ontological reality of evil and to motivate appropriate indignation in response.

These observations underscore the need for a cultural rather than simply an organizational, institutional, or interactional social science. Functional patterning is one thing, the symbolic construction of the meaning of this patterning, and of actors' orientations to it, quite another. At the beginning of the twenty-first century, after Saussure, Wittgenstein, and Geertz, it seems possible finally to entertain this proposition in a serious way. Yet, it remains an idea that has been difficult for social scientists to accept. It has seemed, for many, to undermine the point of a social science, and its very suggestion has aroused controversy. Lévi-Strauss was forced to make a radical break with social anthropology when he insisted that kinship was a linguistic structure, not just a set of institutionally determined social roles: "Exist[ing] only in human consciousness[,] it is an arbitrary system of representations, not the spontaneous development of a real situation" (1963: 31–54). In much the same way and at about the same time, Parsons (most forcefully articulated in Parsons and Shils 1951) seemed to be denying all things sociological when he proclaimed the fundamental analytical distinction between cultural and social systems. Yet, in making these controversial claims, Lévi-Strauss and Parsons were drawing on arguments that were already 50 years old, on semiotics and hermeneutics, respectively. It would take another 50 years before their disciplinary arguments would be taken seriously enough for culture to begin to be given its rightful place.

In the course of recent decades, there has emerged a new recognition of the independent structuring power of culture. It turns out, however, that this new disciplinary self-consciousness has not been any more successful in addressing evil than its reductionist

101

predecessor. In thinking about culture – values and norms, codes and narratives, rituals and symbols – "negativity" has been set off to one side and treated as a residual category. Instead of being systematically addressed, it has been presented as merely a deviation from cultural constructions of the good. In social scientific formulations of culture, a society's "values" are studied primarily as orientations to the good, as efforts to embody ideals.[4] Social notions of evil, badness, and negativity are explored as patterned departures from normatively regulated conduct. If only this were the case! Such a cultural displacement of evil involves moralizing wish-fulfillment, not empirical realism. Not only does it detract from our general understanding of evil, but it makes the relation of evil to modernity much more difficult to comprehend. Thinking of evil as a residual category camouflages the destruction and cruelty that has accompanied enlightened efforts to institutionalize the good and the right. The definition of social evil and the systematic effort to combat it have everywhere accompanied the modern pursuit of reason and progress. That is the central meaning of Foucault's lifework, despite its simplifications, one-sidedness, and undermining relativism. It is the salvageable, saving remnant of the postmodern critique of modernity.

Culturalizing evil is, in sociological terms, every bit as important as efforts to define and institutionalize the good. In semiotic terms (Sahlins 1976), evil is the necessary cognitive contrast to good. In moral terms, exploring heinous evil is the only way to understand and experience the pure and the upright (Caillois 1959).[5] In terms of narrative dynamics (Frye 1957; Propp 1969; Wagner-Pacifici 1986; Smith 2005, 2008), only by creating antiheroes can we implot the dramatic tension between protagonist and antagonist that is transformed by *Bildung* or resolved by catharsis. In ritual terms, it is only the crystallization of evil, with all its stigmatizing and polluting potential, that makes rites of purification culturally necessary and sociologically possible (Turner 1969). Religiously (Lynch 2012), the sacred is incomprehensible without the profane, the promise of salvation meaningless without the threat of damnation. What I am suggesting here, in other words, is that for every value there is an equal and opposite antivalue, for every norm, an antinorm. For every effort to institutionalize comforting and inspiring images of the socially good and right, there is an inter-linked and equally determined effort to construct social evil in horrendous, frightening, and equally realistic ways. Drawing Durkheim back to Nietzsche, and writing under the impact of the trauma of early twentieth-century modernity, Bataille (1985 [1957]: 142–5) made this point in a particularly pungent manner:

> Evil seems to be understandable, but only to the extent to which Good is the key to it. If the luminous intensity of Good did not give the night of Evil its blackness, Evil would lose its appeal. This is a difficult point to understand. Something flinches in him who faces up to it. And yet we know that the strongest effects on the sense are caused by con-trasts . . . Without misfortune, bound to it as shade is to light, indiffer-ences would correspond to happiness. Novels describe suffering, hardly ever satisfaction. The virtue of happiness is ultimately its rarity. Were it easily accessible it would be despised and associated with boredom . . . Would truth be what it is if it did not assert itself gener-ously against falsehood?

Actors, institutions, and societies systematically crystallize and elaborate evil. Most of the time, they do so in pursuit of the good. To this paradoxical and depressing fact, attention must be paid.

The Intellectual Roots of the Displacement of Evil

The truncated, "goodly" conception of culture that so deeply affects contemporary social science is rooted in earlier forms of secular and religious thought.[6] From the Greeks onward, moral philosophy has mostly been oriented to justifying and sustaining the good and to elaborating the requirements of a just society. Plato associated his ideal forms with goodness. To be able to see these forms, he believed, was to be able to act in accordance with morality. In dramatizing Socrates' teachings in *The Republic*, Plato made use of the figure of Thrasymachus to articulate the evil forces threatening ethical life. Rather than suggesting that Thrasymachus embodied bad values, Plato (1965: 18) presented Thrasymachus as denying the existence of values as such: "In all states alike, 'right' has the same meaning, namely what is for the interest of the party established in power, and that is the strongest."

Thrasymachus is an egoist who calculates every action with an eye, not to values, but to the interests of his own person. Plato makes a homology between self/collectivity, interest/value, and evil/good. In doing so, he establishes a set of analogical relationships. Self is to collectivity, as interest is to value, as evil is to good.

Self:collectivity::interest:value::evil:good

The commitment to values is the same as the commitment to collective beliefs, and beliefs and values are the path to the good. Evil should be understood not as the product of bad or negative values, but as the failure to connect to collective values. Evil comes from being self-interested.

In elaborating the republican tradition in political theory, Aristotle (1962: 13) underscored this syllogism, equating a society organized around values with an ethical order: "The best way of life, for individuals severally, as well as for states collectively, is the life of goodness duly equipped with such a store of requisites as makes it possible to share in the activities of goodness."[7] Republics contain virtuous citizens, defined as actors capable of orienting to values outside of themselves. When individuals become oriented to the self rather than the collectivity, republics are endangered; desensitized to values, citizens become hedonistic and materialistic. According to this stark contrast between morality and egoism, value commitments in themselves contribute to the good; evil occurs, not because there are commitments to bad values, but because of a failure to orient to values per se. Hegel continued the Aristotelian contrast between what he called the system of needs and the world of ethical regulation, and pragmatism endorsed the same dichotomy in its own way. For Dewey (1966 [1916]), to value is to value the good. Interpersonal communication produces altruistic normative orientation. Crass materialism and selfishness occur when social structures prevent communication.[8] This philosophical equation of values with goodness and the lack of values with evil informs contemporary communitarianism, which might be described as a marriage between republican and pragmatic thought. Identifying contemporary social problems with egoism and valuelessness, communitarians idealize social values, ignoring the manner in which our values are defined via pejorative contrasts with other values, with others' values, and often with the values of "the other" (see chapter 5 above).

The issue, however, is not values versus interests or having values as compared with not having them. There are always "good" values and "bad." In sociological terms, good values can be crystallized only in relation to values that are feared or considered repugnant. This is not to recommend that values should be relativized in a moral sense, to suggest that they should be "transvalued," or inverted, in Nietzschean terms. It is, rather, to insist that social thinkers recognize how the social construction of evil has been, and remains, empirically necessary for the social commitment to the good.[9]

In the Enlightenment tradition, most forcefully articulated by Kant, concern about the parochial dangers of an Aristotelian "ethics" led to a more abstract and universalistic model of a "moral" as compared to a good society (Alexander 2000a). Nonetheless, one finds in this Kantian tradition the same problem of equating value commitments in themselves with positivity in the normative sense.[10] To be moral is to move from selfishness to the categorical imperative, from self-reference to a collective orientation resting on the ability to put oneself in the place of another. What has changed in Kantianism is not the binary of value-versus-no-value, but the contents of the collective alternative; it has shifted from the ethical to the moral, from the particular and local to the universal and transcendent. The range of value-culture has been expanded and generalized because more substantive and more metaphysical versions came to be seen as particularist, anti-modern, and antidemocratic.

If communitarianism is the contemporary representation of the republican and pragmatic traditions, Habermas's theory of communicative action (1984) represents – for social theory at least – the most influential contemporary articulation of the Kantian approach. Underlying much of Habermas's empirical theory one can find a philosophical anthropology reproducing the simplistic splitting of good and evil. Instrumental, materialistic, and exploitative "labor," for example, is contrasted with altruistic, cooperative, ideal-oriented "communication" (Habermas 1973). These anthropological dichotomies in his early writings are linked in

Habermas's later work (1984) with the sociological contrast between system and lifeworld, the former producing instrumental efficiency, domination, and materialism, the latter producing ideals that make possible equality, community, and morality. According to Habermas's later developmental theory, the capacity for communication and moral self-regulation is enhanced with modernity, which produces such distinctive values as autonomy, solidarity, rationality, and criticism. The possibility of connecting to such values, indeed of maintaining value commitments per se, is impeded by the systems-rationality of modern economic and political life, the materialism of which "colonizes" and undermines the culture-creating, solidarizing possibilities of the lifeworld. In arguing that it is recognition, not communication, that creates value commitments and mutual respect, Axel Honneth (1995) similarly ignores the possibility that pleasurable and cooperative interaction can be promoted by immoral and particularistic values that are destructive of moral communities (Alexander and Pia Lara 1996).

This deracinated approach to culture-as-the-good can be linked to the Western religious traditions of Judaism and Christianity. In order to achieve salvation, the believer must overcome the temptations of the earthly, the material, and the practical to establish transcendental relations with an otherworldly source of goodness. According to this dualistic consciousness, evil is presented as an alternative to the transcendental commitments that establish value. Augustine (1876) describes evil as "the absence of the good"; Aquinas (2003: 70) insists that "evil as such cannot be intended, nor in any way willed or desired, since being desirable has the nature of good, to which evil as such is contrary[,] so we see that no person does any evil except intending something that seems good to the person." The original sin that has marked humanity since the Fall was stimulated by the earthly appetites, by lust rather than idealism and value commitment. It can be redeemed only via a religious consciousness that connects human beings to higher values, either those of an ethical, law-governed community (Judaism) or the moral universalism of a church (Christianity). In this traditional religious universe, evil is connected to non-culture, to passions and figures associated with the earth in contrast with the heavens. Devil symbolism first emerged as a kind of iconographic residual category (Maccoby 1992). Radical Jewish sects created it as a *deus ex machina* to explain the downward spiral of Jewish society, allowing these negative developments to be attributed to forces outside the "authentic" Jewish cultural tradition. This nascent iconography of evil was energetically elaborated by early Christian sects similarly attracted to the possibility of attributing evil to forces outside their own cultural system. The Christian devil was a means of separating the "good religion" of Jesus from the evil (primarily Jewish) forces from which it had emerged.

The Displacement of Evil in Contemporary Social Science

Given these philosophical and religious roots,[11] it is hardly surprising that contemporary social science has conceived culture as composed of values that establish highly esteemed general commitments and norms that create specific moral obligations to pursue the good. Mainstream social scientists and culture critics alike have assumed that a shared commitment to values is positive and beneficial to society. Functionalism was the most striking example of this tendency, and Talcott Parsons its classic representative. According to Parsons, value internalization leads not only to social equilibrium but to mutual respect, solidarity, and cooperation (see chapter 4, above). If common values are not internalized, then the social system is not regulated by value, and social conflict, coercion, and even violence are the probable results. In this sociological version of republicanism, Parsons follows the early- and middle-period Durkheim, who believed that shared values are essential to solidarity and social health. The lack of attachment to values marks the condition Durkheim defined as egoism, and it is by this standard that he defined social pathology. Durkheim emphasized education because he regarded it as the central means for attaching individuals to values. Since the empirical attachment to culture is valued so highly, it is clear that neither Durkheim nor Parsons seriously considered the theoretical or empirical possibility that evil might be valued as energetically as the good.[12]

Sociological folklore pitted functionalist "equilibrium" against "conflict" theory, but Parsonian functionalism was not the only guilty party. Did the theoretical alternatives to functionalism provide a truly different approach to the problem of evil? Let us consider, as a case in point, how Marx conceptualized the depravity of capitalism. Rather than pointing to the social effects of bad values, Marx and Engels argued in *The Communist Manifesto* that capitalism destroyed their very possibility: "All that is holy is profaned, all that is solid melts into air." The structural pressures of capitalism create alienation and egoism; they necessitate an instrumental and strategic action orientation that suppresses values and destroys ideals. Because materialism destroys normativity, there is no possibility for shared understanding, solidarity, or community. Only after socialism removes the devastating forces of capitalist competition and greed will value commitment become possible and solidarity flourish.

The notion that it is not evil values but the absence of values that creates a bad society informs the neo-Marxism of the early Frankfurt School. For Horkheimer and Adorno (1969), late capitalism eliminates authentic values. Culture exists only as an industry; it is a contingent set of expressive symbols, subject to continuous manipulation according to materialistic exigencies. While Habermas's later theory of discourse ethics avoids this kind of mechanism and reduction, it continues to be organized around the pragmatic notion that communicatively generated value commitment leads to mutual understanding, toleration, and solidarity.

The apotheosis of this "critical" approach to evil-as-the-absence-of-value – evil as the displacement of culture by power – is Zygmunt Bauman's explanation of the Holocaust in *Modernity and the Holocaust* (1989). Bauman attributes the social evil of the Holocaust not to motivated cultural action but to the efficiency of the Nazis' bureaucratic killing machine. His explanation does not allow for genocide being caused – as well – by valuations of evil, by general representations of the polluted other that were culturally fundamental to Germany and, more broadly, to Christian society. Yet, only if this possibility is seriously entertained can the Holocaust be seen as an intended action, as something that was desired rather than merely imposed, as an event that grew from systematic tendencies in the culture of modernity. It seems important, morally but also empirically, to emphasize, along with Mosse (1964), Goldhagen (1996), and Herf (1986, 2006), that the Nazis and their masses of German supporters *wanted* to kill Jews. They worked hard to establish Judaism as a symbol of evil and annihilated Jews to purge themselves of this evil in turn. The act of murdering millions of Jewish and non-Jewish people during the Holocaust must be seen as something valued, something desired. It was an evil event motivated not by the absence of values – an absence created by the destructive colonization of lifeworld by economic and bureaucratic systems – but by the presence of heinous values.

Giving Evil its Due: A New Model

We need to elaborate a model of social good and evil that is more complex, more sober, and more realistic than the naturalistic or idealistic models. Symbolically, evil is not a residual category, even if those categorized by it are marginalized socially. From the merely distasteful and sickening to the truly heinous, evil is deeply implicated in the symbolic formulation and institutional maintenance of the good. Because of this, the institutional and cultural vitality of evil must be continuously sustained. The line dividing the sacred from the profane is drawn and redrawn time and time again; this demarcation must retain its vitality, or all is lost.[13] Evil is not only symbolized cognitively, but experienced in a vivid and emotional way (Alexander and Jacobs 1998; Jacobs 2000). Through such phenomena as scandals (Alexander 1987), moral panics (Thompson 1998), public punishments (Smith 1991, 2008), and wars (Smith 2005), societies provide occasions to reexperience and recrystallize the enemies of the good. Wrenching experiences of honor, revulsion, and fear create opportunities for purification that keep what Plato called the memory of justice alive. Only through such direct experiences – provided via interaction or symbolic communication – do members of society come to know evil and to fear it. The emotional-cum-moral catharsis that

Aristotle described as the basis for tragic experience and knowledge is also at the core of knowing and fearing evil (Alexander 2012). Such experiences trigger denunciation of evil in others and confession about evil intentions in oneself, and rituals of punishment and purification in collectivities. In turn, these renew the sacred, the moral, and the good.

Evil is produced, in other words, not simply to maintain domination and power, as Foucault and Marx would argue, but to sustain the possibility of making positive valuations. Evil must be coded, narrated, and embodied in every social sphere – in the intimate sphere of the family, in the world of science, in religion, in the economy, in government, in primary communities. In each sphere, and in every national society, there are deeply elaborated narratives about how evil develops and where it is likely to appear, about epochal struggles that have taken place between evil and the good, and about how good can triumph over evil once again.

This perspective has significant implications for the way we look at both cultural and institutional processes in contemporary societies. I will discuss the former in terms of binary representations and the latter in terms of punishments.

Binary Representations: The Discourse of Civil Society

Civil society refers to the social and cultural bases for political democracy, to the capacity for autonomy and self-regulation that allows independence from coercive political authority.[14] Beyond this broad understanding, civil society is a highly contested concept. It is used both to justify capitalist market relations and to legitimate social movements that oppose and regulate them; some think it refers to everything outside the state, others that it demarcates only the differentiated and universalistic sphere of "public" life. Despite their variation, these approaches agree that civil society indicates a democratic manner of demarcating the good, the moral, the right. When the values of civil society are discussed, they are conceived as referring to qualities and relationships that allow self-regulation and equality. At the basis of this universalistic community, there exists an idealization of the free and autonomous individual who sustains strongly normative commitments to rationality, honesty, responsibility, openness, cooperation, inclusion, and transparency. Action, according to these values, allows individuals and groups to become members of civil society, to be included in its privileges and collective obligations. Whether in the hands of Habermas or Putnam, Cohen or Keane, Fraser or Arato, civil society has been consistently conceptualized in an idealizing way.

My own studies of civil society (Alexander 2006) suggest that the values of civil society are as bad as they are good: its signifiers identify not only the qualities that allow individuals to become members of civil society but the qualities that legitimate their exclusion. The cultural core of civil society is composed not only of codes but of countercodes, antitheses that create meaningful representations for "universalism" and "particularism." On the one side, there is an expansive code that identifies the actors and structures of civil society in terms that promote wider inclusion and increasing respect for individual rights; on the other, there is a restrictive code that identifies actors and structures in terms that focus on ascriptively grounded group identities and promote the exclusion following therefrom. The discourse of civil society is constituted by a continuous struggle among binary codes and among the actors who invoke them, each of whom seeks hegemony over the political field by gaining definitional control over unfolding events.

The binary character of civil culture is demonstrated not simply by the fact that code and countercode are present in every society that aspires to be democratic, but also by the striking circumstance that each code can be defined only in terms of the alternate perspective the other provides. The discourse of civil society revolves around secular salvation. To know how to be part of civil society is to know how one can be socially saved. Members of a society can understand the requirements of social salvation, however, only if they know the criteria for social damnation, for exclusion on the basis of lack of deserts. Just as monotheistic religion divides the world into the saved and the damned, civil discourse divides the world into those who deserve inclusion and those who do not. Members of national communities firmly believe that the world, and this notably includes their own nation, is filled with people who either do not deserve freedom and communal support or are not capable of sustaining them. Members of national communities do not want to save such persons. They do not wish to include them, protect them, or offer them rights, because they conceive them as being unworthy, as in some sense uncivilized.

When citizens make judgments about who should be included in civil society and who should not, about who is a friend and who is an enemy, they draw upon a highly generalized culture structure, a symbolic code that has been in place since the emergence of democratic communities. The basic elements of this structure are sets of homologies, which create likenesses between various terms of social description and prescription, and antipathies, which establish antagonisms between these terms and other sets of symbols. Those who consider themselves worthy members of a national community – as most people do, of course – define themselves in terms of the positive side of this symbolic set; they define those who are not deemed worthy in terms that are established by the negative side. In this sense, it is fair to say that members of the community believe in both the positive and negative sides, that they employ both as viable normative evaluations of political communities. The members of every democratic society consider both symbolic sets as realistic descriptions of individual and social life.

The discourse of civil society rests upon relatively unreflexive assumptions about human nature, which allow the motives of political actors to be clearly conceptualized along with the kind of society they are capable of sustaining. Code and countercode posit human nature in diametrically opposed ways. Because democracy allows self-motivated action, the people who compose it must be described as being capable of activism and autonomy rather than as being passive and dependent. They must be seen as rational and reasonable rather than irrational and hysterical; calm rather than excited; controlled rather than passionate; sane and realistic, not mad or given to fantasy. Democratic discourse, then, posits the following qualities as axiomatic: activism, autonomy, rationality, reasonableness, calm, control, realism, and sanity. The nature of the countercode, the discourse that justifies the

112

restriction of civil society, is clearly implied. If actors are passive and dependent, irrational and hysterical, excitable, passionate, unrealistic, or mad, they cannot be allowed the freedoms of democracy. On the contrary, such persons must be repressed, not only for the sake of civil society but for their own sakes as well.

The Discursive Structure of Social Motives

Democratic code	Counterdemocratic code
activism	passivity
autonomy	dependence
rationality	irrationality
reasonableness	hysteria
calm	excitability
self-control	passion
realism	unreality
sanity	madness

Upon the basis of such contradictory codes about human motives, distinctive representations of social relationships can be built.

Democratically motivated persons will be capable of forming open social relationships rather than secretive ones; they will be trusting rather than suspicious, straightforward rather than calculating, truthful rather than deceitful; their decisions will be based on open deliberation rather than conspiracy, and their attitude toward authority will be critical rather than deferential; in their behavior toward other community members, they will be bound by conscience and honor rather than by greed and self-interest, and they will treat their fellows as friends rather than enemies.

If actors are conceived as counterdemocratic, the social relationships they form will be represented by the second side of these fateful dichotomies. Rather than open and trusting relationships, they will be said to form secret societies premised on suspicion of other human beings. To the authority within these secret societies they will be deferential, but to those outside their tiny group they will behave in a greedy and self-interested way. They will be conspiratorial, deceitful toward others, and calculating in their behavior, conceiving of those outside their group as enemies. If the positive side of this second discourse set describes the symbolic qualities necessary to sustain civil society, the negative side describes a solidary structure in which mutual respect and expansive social integration has broken down.

The Discursive Structure of Social Relationships

Democratic code	Counterdemocratic code
open	secret
trusting	suspicious
critical	deferential
honorable	self-interested
conscience	greed
truthful	deceitful
straightforward	calculating
deliberative	conspiratorial
friend	enemy

Given the discursive structure of motives and civic relationships, it should not be surprising that this set of homologies and antipathies extends to the understanding of social institutions themselves. If members of a national community are depicted as irrational in motive and distrusting in social relationships, they will naturally be represented as creating institutions that are arbitrary rather than regulated by rules; that emphasize brute power rather than law and hierarchy rather than equality; that are exclusive rather than inclusive, and promote personal loyalty over impersonal and contractual obligation; that are regulated by personalities rather than by office obligations, and are organized by faction rather than by groups responsive to the needs of the community as a whole.

The Discursive Structure of Institutions

Democratic code	Counterdemocratic code
rule regulated	arbitrary
law	power
equality	hierarchy
inclusive	exclusive
impersonal	personal
contractual	ascriptive loyalty
social groups	factions
office	personality

When they are presented in their simple binary forms, these cultural codes appear schematic. In fact, they reveal the skeletal structures upon which social communities build the familiar stories that guide their everyday taken-for-granted political life. The positive side of these structured sets provides elements for the comforting and inspiring story of a democratic, free, and spontaneously integrated social order, civil society in an ideal sense. The structure and narrative of political virtue form the "discourse of liberty." The discourse is embodied in the great and the little stories that democratic nations tell about themselves. The American story about George Washington and the cherry tree highlights honesty and virtue; English accounts of the "Battle of Britain" reveal the courage, self-sufficiency, and spontaneous cooperation of the British in contrast to the villainous forces of Hitlerian Germany; French legends about the honorable, trusting, and independent patriots who resisted the Nazi occupation underlay the construction of the Fourth Republic after World War II.

The elements on the negative side of these symbolic sets are also tightly intertwined. They provide the categories for the plethora of stories that permeate democratic understanding of the repugnant sides of community life. Taken together, these form a "discourse of repression." If people are not represented as having the capacity for reason, if they cannot rationally process information and cannot tell truth from falseness, then they will be loyal to leaders for purely personal reasons and easily manipulated in turn. Because such persons are ruled by calculation rather than by conscience, they are without the honor that is critical in democratic affairs. Constructing people in terms of such anticivil qualities makes it necessary that they be denied access to rights and the protection of law. If they have the capacity for neither voluntary nor responsible behavior, these marginal members of the community – those who are unfortunate enough to be constructed under the counterdemocratic code – must ultimately be repressed. They cannot be regulated by law, nor will they accept the discipline of office. Their loyalties can be only familial and particularistic. The institutional and legal boundaries of civil society, it is feared, can provide no bulwark against their lust for personal power.

The positive side of this discursive formation is viewed by the members of democratic communities as a source not only of purity but of purification. The discourse of liberty is taken to sum up the best in a civil community, and its tenets are considered sacred. The objects that the discourse creates seem to possess an awesome power that places them at the center of society, a location – sometimes geographical, often stratificational, always symbolic – that compels their defense at almost any cost. The negative side of this symbolic formation is viewed as profane. Representing the worst in the national community, it embodies evil. The objects it identifies threaten the core community from somewhere outside. From this marginal position, they present powerful sources of pollution. To be close to these polluted objects is dangerous. Not only can one's reputation be sullied and one's status endangered, but one's security as well. To have one's self or movement identified in terms of these objects causes anguish, disgust, and alarm. This code is taken to be a threat to the center of civil society itself.

For contemporary Americans, the categories of the pure and polluted discourses seem natural and fully historical. Democratic law and procedures are seen as having been won by the founding fathers and guaranteed by documents like the Bill of Rights and the Constitution. The qualities of the repressive code are embodied, with equal verisimilitude, in the dark visions of tyranny and lawlessness, whether embodied by eighteenth-century British monarchs, twentieth-century Soviet communists, or twenty-first century Islamists. Pulp fiction and highbrow drama counterpose these dangers with compelling images of the good. When works of the imagination represent this discursive formation in powerfully evocative ways, they become contemporary classics. For the generation that matured during World War II, George Orwell's *1984* made the discourse of repression emblematic of the struggles of their time.

Some events are so gross or so sublime that they generate almost immediate consensus about how these symbolic sets should be applied. For most members of a national community, great national wars clearly demarcate the good and the bad. The nation's soldiers are the embodiments of the discourse of liberty; the foreign nations and soldiers who oppose them represent some potent combination

116

of the counterdemocratic code. In the course of American history, this negative code has been extended to a vast and variegated group, to the British, native peoples, pirates, the South and the North, Africans, old European nations, fascists, Communists, Germans, Japanese, Vietnamese, and Iraqis. Identification in terms of the discourse of repression is essential for vengeful combat to be pursued. Once this polluting discourse is applied, it becomes impossible for good people to reason with those on the other side. If one's opponents are beyond reason, deceived by leaders who operate in secret, the only option is to read them out of the human race. When great wars are successful, they provide powerful narratives that dominate the nation's postwar life. Hitler and Nazism have formed the backbone of a huge array of Western myths and stories, providing master metaphors for everything from profound discussions about the Final Solution to the good guy/bad guy plots of television dramas and situation comedies.

For most events, however, discursive identity is contested. Social confrontations are about how to distribute actors across the structure of this discourse, for there is no determined relationship between any event or group and either side of the cultural scheme. Actors struggle to taint one another with a repressive brush and to wrap themselves in the rhetoric of liberty. In periods of tension and crisis, social struggles becomes a matter of how far and to whom the discourses of liberty and repression apply. The causes of victory and defeat, imprisonment and freedom, and sometimes even of life and death, are often discursive domination, which depends upon how popular narratives about good and evil are extended. Is it protesting students who are like Nazis, or the conservatives who try to punish them? Are the members of the Communist Party considered to be fascistic, or the members of the House Un-American Activities Committee pursuing them? When Watergate began, only the actual burglars were called conspirators and polluted by the discourse of repression. George McGovern and his fellow Democrats were unsuccessful in their efforts to apply this discourse to the White House, the executive staff, and the Republican Party, elements of civil society that succeeded in maintaining their identity in liberal terms (Alexander 1987). At a later point in the crisis, such a reassuring relationship to the culture structure no longer held. The general discursive structure, in other words, is used to legitimate friends and delegitimate opponents in the course of real historical time.

Punishment: Social Process and Institutions

If the cultural dimension of society as organized around evil as much as around good, this does not imply social evil can be understood simply in discursive terms. On the contrary, organizations, power, and face-to-face confrontations are critical in determining how and to whom binary representations of good and evil are applied. They determine what the "real" social effects of evil will be in time and space.

The social processes and institutional forces that specify and apply representations about the reality of evil can be termed punishment. In *The Division of Labor in Society* (1984 [1893]), Durkheim first suggested that crime is normal and necessary because it is only punishment that allows society to separate what it considers normative from deviant behavior. From the perspective developed here, punishment is the social medium through which the practices of actors, groups, and institutions are meaningfully and effectively related to the category of evil. It is through punishment that evil is naturalized. Punishment essentializes evil, making it appear to emerge from actual behaviors and identities, rather than being culturally and socially imposed upon them.

Punishment takes both routine and spontaneous forms (Smith 2008). The bureaucratic iterations of evil are called crimes. In organizational terms, the situational references of criminal acts are precisely defined by civil and criminal law, whose relevance to particular situations is firmly decided by courts and police. Polluting contact with civil law brings monetary sanctions; stigmatization by contact with criminal law brings incarceration, radical social isolation, and sometimes even death.

The nonroutine iterations of evil are less widely understood and appreciated. They refer to processes of stigmatization rather than to crimes (Goffman 1963; Steiner 1956). What Cohen (1972) first identified as moral panics represent fluid, rapidly formed crystallizations of evil in relation to unexpected events, actors, and institutions. Historical witch trials (Erickson 1966; Reed 2007) and more contemporary anticommunist witch hunts, for example, are stimulated by the sudden experience of weakness in group boundaries. Panics over crime waves, by contrast, develop in response to the chaotic and disorganizing entrance of new, formerly disreputable social actors into civil society. Whatever their specific cause, and despite their evident irrationality, moral panics have powerful effect. Focusing on new sources of evil, they draw an exaggerated line between social pollution and the good. This cultural clarification prepares the path for a purging organizational response, for trials of transgressors, for expulsion, and incarceration.

Scandals represent a less ephemeral but still nonroutine form of social punishment. Scandals are public degradations of individuals and groups for behavior considered polluting to their status or office. In order to maintain the separation between good and evil, the behavior of an individual or group is "clarified" by symbolizing it as having shifted from purity to danger. The religious background of Western civil society makes such declension typically appear as a fall from grace, as a personal sin, a lapse created by individual corruption and the loss of individual responsibility. In the discourse of civil society, the greatest sins are associated with deceit and selfishness, and the inability to maintain autonomy and independence. Scandal is created because civil society demands continual revivifications of social evil. These rituals of degradation range from apparently trivial gossip sheets to the kinds of deeply serious, civil-religious events that create national convulsions. The Dreyfus affair that threatened to undermine the Third Republic in France and the Watergate affair that toppled the Nixon regime in the United States represented efforts to crystallize and punish social evil on this systematic level. Scandals, like moral panics, have not only cultural but fundamental institutional effects, repercussions that range from the removal of specific persons from status or office to deep and systematic changes in organizational structure and regime.

There is nothing fixed or determined about scandals and moral panics. Lines of cultural demarcation are necessary but not sufficient to their creation. Whether or not this or that individual or group becomes punished is the outcome of struggles for cultural power, struggles that depend on shifting coalitions and the mobilization of resources of a material and not only ideal kind (Mast 2012). This applies not only to the creation of panics and scandals but to their denouements. They are terminated by purification rituals reestablishing the sharp line between evil and good, a transition made possible by the act of punishment.

Transgression and the Affirmation of Evil and Good

The "autonomy" of evil, culturally and institutionally, allows the experience and practice of evil to become not only frightening and repulsive but desirable. The social creation of evil results not only in efforts to avoid evil but also in the pursuit of it. Rather than a negative that directs people toward the good, social evil can be pursued as an end in itself. As Bataille observed, "evil is always the object of an ambiguous condemnation"; it is "not only the dream of the wicked" but "to some extent the dream of [the] Good" (1985 [1957]: 29, 21). Attraction to the idea and experience of evil motivates widespread practices of transgression, what Foucault, following Bataille, termed "limit experiences" (Miller 1993).[15]

> *Sacred* simultaneously has two contradictory meanings . . . The taboo gives a negative definition of the sacred object and inspires us with awe . . . Men are swayed by two simultaneous emotions: they are driven away by terror and drawn by an awed fascination. Taboo and transgression reflect these two contradictory urges. The taboo would forbid the transgression but the fascination compels it . . . The sacred aspect of taboo is what draws men towards it and transfigures the original interdiction. (Bataille 1986 [1957]: 68, emphasis in original)

When evil becomes positively evaluated, it creates a kind of inverted liminality. Transgression takes place when actions, associations, and rhetoric – practices that would typically be defined and sanctioned as serious threats to the good – become objects of desire and sometimes even social legitimation. Bataille believed that transgression occurs mainly in the cultural imagination, of literature, although he also wrote extensively about eroticism and the dark social developments of the early and mid-century period

120

– Nazism, war, and Stalinism (cf. Giesen 2011).[16] Transgression also, however, takes on decidedly social-structural form. In criminal activity and popular culture, evil provides the basis of complex social institutions that provide highly sought after social roles, careers, and personal identities. Jack Katz (1988) investigated transgression in his phenomenological reconstruction of the "badass syndrome,"[17] as did Richard Strivers (1982) in his discussion of the apocalyptic dimension of 1960s rock and roll. The latter embodied the noir strain of popular culture that later transmogrified into the "bad rapper" phenomenon.

Social thinkers and artists who explore the attractions of the dark side, whether via moral imagination or aesthetic action, risk being tarred by representatives of social morality with a polluting brush. Such knee-jerk responses confuse causes with effects. Societies construct evil so there can be punishment, for it is the construction and response to evil that defines and revivifies the good. One should not, then, mistake the aesthetic imagining of evil, the vicarious experiencing of evil, or the intellectual exploration of evil for the actual practice of evil itself.

Modern and postmodern societies have been beset by a socially righteous fundamentalism, both religious and secular. Moralists wish to purge the cultural imagination of references to eros and violence; they condemn frank discussions of transgressive desires and actions in schools and other public places; they seek to punish and sometimes even to incarcerate those who practice victimless crimes on the grounds that they violate the collective moral conscience. The irony is that, without the imagination and the social identification of evil, there would be no possibility for the attachment to the good that moralists wish so vehemently to defend. Rather than undermining conventional morality, transgression underlines it. Bataille, whom James Miller (1993) called the *philosophe maudit* of French intellectual life, insisted upon this point:

> Transgression has nothing to do with the primal liberty of animal life. It opens the door into what lies beyond the limits usually observed, but it maintains these limits just the same. Transgression is complementary to the profane world, exceeding its limits but not destroying it. (Bataille 1986 [1957]: 68)

Figure 6.1: Amnesty International logo

Amnesty International, winner of the Nobel Peace Prize and one of the world's most effective nongovernmental democratic organizations, exposes and mobilizes opposition to torture and other repressive governmental practices. At the heart of the internal and external discourse of this prototypically do-gooder organization, one finds an obsessive concern with defining, exploring, and graphically presenting evil, the success of which allows members and outsiders vicariously to experience evil's physical and emotional effects.[18] In the Amnesty logo, good and evil are tensely intertwined (see figure 6.1). At the core is a candle, representing the fervent attention, patience, and sacrality of Amnesty's commitment to life. Surrounding the candle is barbed wire, indicating concentration camps and torture.

This binary structure is iterated throughout the persuasive documents that Amnesty distributes to the public and in the talk of Amnesty activists themselves. These revolve around narratives that portray in graphic, often gothic detail the heinous things inflicted upon innocent people and portray, in a tone of almost uncomprehending awe, the ability of prisoners to endure unspeakable suffering while remaining, even at the point of death, caring, and dignified human beings. Amnesty's attention to evil, to constructing the oppressor and graphically detailing its actions, contributes to maintaining the ideals of moral justice and sacralizing the human spirit, not only in thought but in practice.

It is in order to explain and illuminate such a paradox that a sociology of evil must be born.

— 7 —

DE-CIVILIZING THE CIVIL SPHERE

Theories of modernization, development and rationalization have assumed that broader solidary structures are created in the course of social development, as offshoots of other, more visible and more familiar structural processes such as urbanization, marketization, socialization, bureaucratization, and secularization. I would argue, to the contrary, that the construction of a wider and more inclusive sphere of solidarity needs to be studied in itself (Alexander 2006).[1] From the beginning of its appearance in human societies, civil society has been organized, insofar as it has been organized at all, around its own particular cultural codes (see chapter 6, above). It has been able to broadcast its idealized image of social relationships because it has been organized by certain kinds of communicative institutions, and departures from these relationships have been sanctioned or rewarded in more material terms by certain kinds of regulative institutions. Civil society has been sustained, as well, by distinctive personality structures and by forms of interaction that are of an unusual kind.

In thinking about such an independent sphere of civil solidarity, the social theorist must walk a delicate line. The codes, institutions, and interactions that compose such a sphere must be considered in themselves, as structures in their own right. Their status cannot simply be read off from the condition of the spheres which surround civil society; they are not simply dependent variables. At the same time, the briefest consideration makes it clear that, in a concrete sense, these internal modes of organization are always deeply interpenetrated with the rest of society. At every point they are connected to activities in other spheres. They reach out beyond civil society narrowly conceived to set standards and create images in other spheres. Conversely, what happens in other spheres of society – what they make possible and what they foreclose – has fundamental effects on the structure and operation of culture, institutions, and interactions in civil society.

Indeed, the tension between what might be called the internal and external references of civil society is not merely a theoretical issue; it is of central empirical and ideological concern. To the degree that civil society gains autonomy from other spheres, to that degree it can define social relationships in a more consistently universalistic way. The binary structure of the discourse of civil society suggests, however, that, even in the most ideal circumstances, such universalism can never be achieved in anything more than a highly proximate way. Because social reality is far from ideal, moreover, the autonomy of civil society normally is continually compromised and reduced. The exigencies of non-civil spheres, institutions and modes of interaction permeate civil society, with the result that the discourse of repression is applied far and wide. The world of the "we" becomes narrowed; the world of the "they" becomes larger and assumes multifarious forms. It is not only groups outside the nation-state that are disqualified from gaining entrance to civil society, but many groups inside it as well.

It is to a systematic model of these boundary processes that I devote this chapter. In this task, idealizing approaches to civility and the public sphere will not be of much help. Whether critical or apologetic, such approaches have suggested that civil society should be able to stand on its own and eliminate the influence of these other spheres: otherwise it will not be able to stand at all. From Aristotle and Rousseau to Arendt and Habermas, idealistic thinkers have embraced the utopianism of civil society, not only as a regulating idea, or norm, but as a possible expression of the social whole. They have argued that it is possible to create a social system that is thoroughly civil, solidaristic, altruistic, and inclusive; a social system, in other words, homologous with civil society itself. They have dismissed the economic world as the world of necessity, one from which normative ideas of reciprocity are

124

excluded *tout court*. They have rejected the political world as inherently bureaucratic and instrumental, as resting always and everywhere on domination alone. These "systems" are conceived as inherently uncivil, as colonizers of the lifeworld of a solidary sphere that is doomed because of its vulnerability to spheres of a more material kind. The civil is also seen as weak vis-à-vis the religious sphere, which can squelch the open-ended and universalistic dialogue that marks civil understanding.

Such idealizing approaches make forceful criticisms of non-civil spheres, and I make generous use of their criticisms in my discussion below. They err, however, by ignoring the necessity for differentiation and complexity, not only institutionally but morally. The more developed a society, the more there emerge different kinds of institutional spheres and discourses. The reach and scope of civil society is restricted by these other spheres; at the same time, however, the civil sphere enters into institutional and moral interchanges with these other worlds. Interpenetration cuts both ways: civil society can colonize these other spheres; it is not simply colonized *by* them. To avoid the idealist fallacy, we must recognize that civil society is always nested in the practical worlds of uncivil spheres, and we must study the compromises and fragmentations, the "real" rather than merely idealized civil society, that results (Alexander 1998c).

Civil society is instantiated in the real because social systems exist in real space, because they have been constructed in real time, and because they must perform functions that go beyond the construction of solidarity itself. Instantiation reduces the ideal of equal and free participation – it compromises and fragments the potentially civil sphere – by attaching status to "primordial" qualities that have nothing to do with one's position in civil society as such. Primordial qualities are those attributed to persons by virtue of their membership in a particular group, one that is thought to be based on unique characteristics those outside the group can, by definition, never hope to attain. Such qualities can be analogized to physical attributes like race and blood; but almost any social attribute can assume a primordial position. Language, race, national origins, religion, class, intelligence, and region – all these have been primordialized at historical conjunctures. In different times and in different places, actors have become convinced that only those possessing certain versions of these qualities have what it takes to become members of civil society. They have believed that individuals and groups who do not possess these qualities are uncivilized and cannot be included. "Civil" in this way becomes contrasted with "primordial." The truth, of course, is that the very introduction of particular criteria is uncivil. Civil primordiality is a contradiction in terms.

Space: The Geography of Civil Society

Civil society is idealized, by philosophers and by lay members alike, as a universalistic and abstract space, an open world without limits, an endless horizon. In fact, however, territory is basic to any real existing historical society. Territory converts the space of civil society into a particular place. Civil society can become unique and meaningful only as a particular place. It is not just some place, or any place, but our place, a center that is different from places outside its territory. Attachment to this central place becomes primordialized. As it becomes a primordial quality, territory divides; it becomes articulated with the binary discourse of civil society. The capacity for liberty becomes limited to those who have their feet on the sacred land, and the institutions and interaction of civil society become distorted and segmented in turn.

Nationalism can be conceived as the pollution of space demarcated by the territorial limits of states. Civility had, of course, always been circumscribed by centers, but before the sixteenth century these primordial territories were constructed more locally, as villages, cities, regions, or simply as the physical areas inhabited by extended kinship networks and tribes. Beginning in the Renaissance, territory began to be viewed nationally. Attachment to one's place meant connection to the land of the nation. It is important to see that this geographical bifurcation was held to be true no matter how the national territory was defined, whether a national community of language and blood, as in the German case, or an abstract universal community of ideas, as in post-revolutionary France. Only members of this nation were seen as capable of

126

reason, honesty, openness, and civility; members of other nations were not. Membership in other national territories seemed to generate dishonesty, distrust, and secrecy. They were naturally enemies.

This restriction on universalism has had extraordinary consequences for the real history of civil societies. One has been the continuous intertwining of real civil societies and war, the ultimate expression of relationships of an uncivil kind. Kant believed that democracies would never make war on other democracies; he suggested that the qualities of universalism and reason that characterized such societies would incline them to dialogue rather than force and would make it difficult for them to stereotype and brutalize people on the other side. But the democratic quality of other nations is always something open to debate, and the territorial bifurcation of civil charisma makes the civility of others much more difficult to discern. This explains why, throughout the history of civil societies, war has been a sacred obligation; to wage war against members of other territories has been simultaneously a national and a civilizing task. Ancient Athens, the first real if limited democracy, whose polis has formed the model for civil societies until today, waged continuous war against its neighboring city states, fighting against the barbarism that "foreign" territory implied. For the Renaissance city states in Italy, military glory was a central virtue, and their publics defended and extended their civil societies by waging war against "foreign," yet equally civil communities in their national clime. The imperial expansion of Northern European nations from the sixteenth through to the nineteenth centuries certainly had economic motives; but it was inspired, as well, by the urgent need to civilize enemies of civilization not fortunate enough to be nurtured in the same part of the earth as they.

But it is the great "imperial republics," as Raymond Aron called them, that demonstrate this territorial bifurcation of civility in the most striking way. When the English and French fought against each other from the sixteenth through to the nineteenth centuries, they were societies that resembled each other in fundamental ways, each considering itself to possess a civil, if not democratic, dimension of social life. Yet elites and common people alike were in each nation convinced that it was only their national territories that allowed them to breathe free. Were the motives of Napoleonic France any different in their wars of forced national liberation, which placed in the same polluted categories the "enslaved" citizens of nations as diverse as Egypt and Germany, not to mention Italy and England itself? And then there is the centuries long military history of the democratic United States, whose every war has been fought as a ritual sacrifice so that the oppressed of other countries may become Americanized, and thus free. This is not to say that many of these above named wars have not, in fact, been exercises in self-defense or national liberation. It is to suggest, however, that the connection between national territory and the binary discourse of civil societies has been striking indeed, and that it has always and everywhere inspired wars of an atrocious and punitive kind.

The nationalist understanding of civility has also had fragmenting consequences of an internal kind. It has allowed those excluded from civil society to be constructed as foreigners and aligned with the territorial enemies against whom wars are waged. Those who are excluded are often seen, in other words, not only as uncivil but as genuine threats to national security. In America, this has taken the form of nativism, defined by John Higham as the "intense opposition to an internal minority on the grounds of its foreign connection" (1992). In the course of American history, virtually every immigrant group has been subject to this construction, from Indians to African Americans, from Catholic immigrants to Jews, from Germans in World War I to Japanese in World War II, to Islamic immigrants after 9/11. There is no need to multiply examples of this kind, or to explain how French anti-Semitism turned Dreyfus into a German spy and German Nazism turned the Jewish "nation" into the international capitalist conspiracy threatening the independence of the German state. Such facts are well known, but their theoretical implications are not well understood.

Because civil society is territorial and spatially fixed, it produces its own enemies. Even in the most civil of societies, the discourse of liberty is bifurcated in a territorial manner. In making pollution primordial, this bifurcation makes repression more likely. This is why, in their quest for participation in the world of civil society, the excluded so often try to represent themselves as patriots.

128

During the rise of German anti-Semitism in Weimar, Jewish organizations widely publicized the fact that tens of thousands of their
compatriots had died for the Kaiser. Throughout their long struggle for inclusion, champions of the African-American community
have pointed proudly to the fact that blacks have fought willingly
in every major American war, beginning with the Revolution itself.
According to T.H. Marshall, it was the patriotic participation of
the British working class in World War II that created the cross-
class solidarity that formed the basis for postwar creation of the
welfare state.

If nationalism restricts civility by bifurcating space outside the
nation, regionalism recreates a similar if sometimes less violent
restriction for space within the nation. It is not only nations that
are centers, but also, very conspicuously, particular cities and
regions within them. These domestic centers primordialize the
discourse of liberty, constructing the periphery as lacking the charisma of national civility, as a kind of foreign territory inside the
nation itself. City and country was for centuries one of the most
pernicious distinctions of this kind. The German burgher proverb,
"the city air makes us free," was intended to be much more than
a sociological observation about the effects of legal rights.
Throughout the history of European civil societies, peasants were
likened to animals or, in Marx's inimitable phrase, to lumps of
clay. Regional divisions like North and South, and East and West,
have always and everywhere carried a surplus of meaning. Such
regional divisions have fragmented the civil society of nations, its
culture, its interactions, and often its regulative and communicative institutions. When they have overlapped with other kinds of
exclusions – economic, ethnic, political, or religious – they have
formed the basis for repressive closure movements, for the construction of ghettos, for brutal and aggressive exercises in forced
incorporation, for secessionist movements and civil wars.

Time: Civil Society as Historical Sedimentation

Just as civil societies are always created in real space, so they are
created in real time. The utopia of civility suggests a timeless realm

where people have always been thus, and always will be. Yet every civil society has actually been started, by somebody, at a particular time; and in virtually every territorial space different regimes of more and less civil societies have been started over and over again.

What is important about this temporality is that it becomes primordialized. The time of origin of a community is treated as a sacred time, mythologized in national narratives and replicated by periodic rituals of remembrance. The founders of such a community are sacralized as well. A charisma of time attaches to the founders of civil societies, who were there "at the beginning." Myths of origins not only give to these founders pride of place, but they attribute their accomplishment to the primordial characteristics of this founding group: to their religion, their race, their class, their language, to their country of origin if it is different from the nation they founded at a later time. The origins of myths of civil society narrate the founders' role in terms of the discourse of liberty, but the capacity for liberty is temporalized. Only the primordial characteristics of the founding group, it is widely believed, allowed them to succeed in founding the national society at such a propitious historical time.

If the characteristics of the founders are equated with the pure categories of civil society, it is only logical – in a cultural sense – that the qualities of those who come after them, insofar as they differ from the founders' own, should be equated with the impure categories of this civil discourse. Temporality creates a time order of civility, a rank order of categorical qualities that become the basis for claims of privilege within civil society itself. In American history, each new immigrant group has been considered polluted in crucial respects. The inability to speak English properly has been attributed to an incapacity for rationality and clarity. The extended kinship networks that typify early forms of ethnic communities have been seen as a manifestation of closed rather than open behavior, as breeding factionalism rather than open competition, as manifestations of secrecy rather than openness and trust. Different religious practices are invariably considered to be inferior ones, characterized in terms of emotionality rather than control and hierarchy rather than equality. The result is not simply discrimination but repulsion and fear. There is the suspicion that these later arriving groups are outside the very categories of civil society itself. Can the newly arrived Irish immigrants ever become good Americans? Can Jews? Can the newly arrived immigrants from China, Japan, Mexico, Somalia, and Iraq? How can this be possible, if they are so different from us?

Yet, if staggered arrival creates bifurcations, the passing of time can blur them. Ethnic succession is not simply an economic fact, created by ecological and material pressures that allow one group to leave a niche and another to enter it. It is a cultural learning process that may be tempered by time. Familiarity does not lead to understanding exactly; rather, it leads to identification, a process that interpolates both space and time. Long-term presence in the primordial place often cleanses and purifies primordial qualities, allowing what were once considered fundamentally different characteristics to be seen, instead, as variations on a common theme. This is not an evolutionary process that happens automatically (see chapter 4, above). Bridging, connecting, and transversing are projects carried forward by temporally disprivileged groups. Making use of the communicative and the regulatory institutions of civil society, they demand to be reconsidered in more civil terms. In "ethnic" fiction, writers represent their group's primordial qualities in terms of the "common tradition," in both an aesthetic and a moral sense. They offer alternative framings of primordial traits, using humor, tragedy, or romance to allay danger and create a sense of familiarity. Immigrant social movements and well-known immigrant personalities present themselves as embodying traditional civil qualities. They argue that they are revivifying the national discourse of liberty, and that their ethnic qualities present complementary analogs of the characteristics exhibited by the founding groups.

To understand fully the implications of temporality, one must see that the origins of a civil community are also reconstructed in a manner that is much less voluntaristic than the pacific quality of "immigration" implies. The temporal concreteness of civil societies means that their foundings interrupted and displaced already existing social arrangements. They may have emerged from revolutionary upheavals against a more conservative or more radical regime; they may have been founded upon the military conquest

131

of native peoples or resident national groups; they may have involved domination via purchase through commercial treaties or through political acquisition of a less direct type. When the radical English parliament organized its political revolution against kingship, it did not merely emphasize the expansion of civil society; rather, it presented its revolution as a victory of a different ethnic group, the Anglo-Saxons, over the Royalist blood line. The French revolutionaries did not only make a universal and democratic insurrection, but they proclaimed a victory for the Gauls over the Francs. The American Revolution also involved temporal displacement, not only victory over the Native American aboriginal peoples but over ethnic peoples who were not Anglo-Saxon in type. Whatever the specific manner of displacement, the primordial characteristics of the dominated group are stigmatized; they are represented in terms of impure categories of the triumphant civil state. Civil society is, at its very origins, fragmented and distorted in what are often heinous ways.

These distorted self-understandings of civil society set off chain reactions that often invite "refoundings" of an equally violent type. The repercussions of such posterior reconstructions can produce physical displacement and ghettoization. Apartheid in South Africa occurred after the Afrikaner "refounding" of the earlier settler society founded by the English, and that nation, after the end of Apartheid, is in the process of being refounded – this time by black Africans again. When the Nazis refounded Germany as an Aryan and Christian state, this involved not merely physical displacement and coercion but mass extermination. Refoundings can produce centuries of struggles for liberation and oppression, which often lead to civil war, as did America's racial caste system, which was intrinsic to the founding of a civil society of an otherwise profoundly democratic type.

The temporal bifurcations of civil societies intertwine with fragmentations founded on territory, particularly because both involve constructions that refer to the founding of nations. The primordial qualities that societies identify with liberty refer to founders who were "there at the beginning." When excluded national groups represent themselves as patriots, as people whose contributions to national security have been unfairly ignored, they are not only symbolically inserting themselves into the particular place of the nation but also into its historical time. Because historical memory preserves the charisma of time, it is always disputed by groups who are temporally displaced. Originating events, and later critical historical ones as well, are continually reconstituted in order to legitimate a new primordial definition of civility. Groups who have been excluded or dominated reconstrue their nation's history so that civility is described in broader and more expansive ways, and threatened core groups try to maintain restrictive primordial definitions or even to make them narrower still. Social movements use communicative institutions to convince the public that history must be revised; they use regulatory institutions to make illegal the norms that are implied by this outmoded version of history.

Function: The Destruction of Boundary Relations and Their Repair

Societies are more than collectivities framed by time and rooted in space. They are enormously complex social systems whose institutions become increasingly specialized, separated from one another not only by the differentiation of their physical organization and staff, but also by the normative understandings that inform and regulate them. The possibility of institutional and cultural differentiation into increasingly separate spheres lies at the very heart of the critical theory of modernity I am developing here. The civil sphere's capacity for justice, for equality and liberty, depends upon the creation of a space that can stand outside spheres of a more restrictive kind. Yet, this autonomy must be understood in a dialectical way. The very independence that makes civil society possible also makes it vulnerable.

There is a dangerous and fundamentally illusory theoretical tendency to see functional differentiation as a process that creates stability and individuation. Functional differentiation may be integrative and ennobling, but it is by no means necessarily so. If the solidarity and universalism of civil society form one dimension of a modern social system, these qualities are challenged by spheres abutting civil society which have radically different functional

133

concerns – which operate according to contradictory goals, employ different kinds of media, and produce social relations of an altogether different sort. The goal of the economic sphere is wealth, not justice in the civil sense; it is organized around efficiency, not solidarity, and depends upon hierarchy, not equality, to produce its goals. Polities produce power, not reciprocity; they depend upon authority, not independence; they demand loyalty, not criticism, and seek to exercise coercive, if legitimate, forms of social control. The religious sphere produces salvation, not worldly just deserts; it is premised upon a fundamental inequality, not only between God and merely human believers but between God's representatives – his shepherds and those they guide and instruct on earth; and no matter how radically egalitarian or reformed the message, the very transcendental character of religious relationships demands mystery and deference, not reciprocity or dialogue of a transparent kind. In the family, the species is reproduced in a biological and a moral sense; it is organized around eros and love, not, in the first instance, self-control and questioning; its organization depends upon deference in a fundamental way.

Each of these non-civil spheres creates specifically functional kinds of inequalities. Fathers historically assumed power over women and children in families; property-owners and professional managers organize, lead, and command economic workers; politicians and bureaucrats exercise domination over those who do not hold office in the state; religious notables whether priests, rabbis, or imams, act authoritatively vis-à-vis lay people in their congregations. These privileged accumulations of power may be considered as usurpations, but they are not necessarily so. Certainly, it is difficult to conceive how such noncivil spheres could operate in an independent or effective fashion without specialized experts whose authority allowed them to co-ordinate and direct institutional relations – which means, in fact, to "govern" in some way. It is possible to conceive of just and legitimate forms of such inequalities, insofar as the power over goods and process is acquired by persons with distinctive insights and effectively specialized skills.

The problem is that privileged accumulations in these other spheres, to one degree or another, routinely and systematically become translated into the sphere of civil society itself (Walzer

134

1983). So do the particular goods upon which these accumulations of power are based. These goods themselves possess a distinctive charisma, as do the powers that have the authority to speak and act in their name. Money is important, not only because of its instrumental power but also because its possession is typically taken to represent a distinctive and respected achievement in the world of economic life. Grace in the sphere of salvation, patriarchal authority in the family, and power in the political sphere should be understood in similar ways. Yet, as a result of this charisma, these qualities become represented not merely as prestigious possessions acquired in specialized spheres, but as qualities that mean something in civil society itself. Stratification in these other spheres becomes translated into the bifurcating discourse of civil society. To be rich, for example, often seems to suggest moral goodness; insofar as it does, it is translated into the discourse of liberty. To be poor, on the other hand, often exposes one to degradation, to constructions that pollute one in various ways. In one sense this translation is complicated: it involves analogical chains between different semiotic codes, metaphorical transformations and narratives that establish homologous relationships between motives, relations, and institutions in different walks of life. In another sense, the translation is very simple. The privileged accumulations of goods in non-civil spheres are used to achieve power and recognition in civil society, to gain access to its discourse and control over its institutions, and to re-represent the elites of other spheres as ideal participants in the interactive processes of civil life.

These boundary relationships can be conceived in terms of facilitating inputs, destructive intrusions, and civil repairs. Boundary tensions can seriously distort civil society, threatening the very possibility for an effective and democratic social life. These distorting forces are seen as destructive intrusions; in the face of them, civil society makes repairs by seeking to regulate and reform what happens in non-civil spheres. Yet such subsystem interpenetration can also go the other way. The goods and norms of other spheres can be seen as facilitating the realization of a more civil life. Conservative theorists and politicians, not to mention the elites in these non-civil spheres themselves, are inclined to emphasize the facilitating inputs of non-civil spheres to the creation of a good social life. Those on the liberal and radical left are more inclined to see such interpenetrations as destructive intrusions, and to demand civil repairs be made as a result. Neither side of this argument can be ignored in the effort to develop a critical perspective on modern life.

That the economic sphere can facilitate the construction of a civil sphere is an historical and sociological fact. When an economy is structured by markets, behavior is encouraged to be independent, rational, and self-controlled. It was for this reason that the early intellectuals of capitalism, from Montesquieu to Adam Smith, hailed market societies as a calm and civilizing antidote to the militaristic glories of aristocratic life. It is in part for this same reason that post-Communist societies have staked their emerging democracies on the construction of market economies. Yet, quite apart from markets, industrialization itself can be seen in a positive vein. By creating an enormous supply of cheap and widely available material media, mass production lessens the invidious distinctions of status-markers that separated rich and poor in more restricted economies. It becomes increasingly possible for masses of people to express their individuality, their autonomy, and their equality through consumption and, in so doing, to partake of the common symbolic inheritance of modern cultural life. Facilitating inputs are produced from the production side as well. As Marx himself pointed out, the complex forms of teamwork and cooperation demanded by productive enterprises can be considered forms of socialization through which persons learn to respect and trust their fellow partners in the civil sphere.

Insofar as the economy supplies the civil sphere with facilities like independence, self-control, rationality, equality, self-realization, cooperation, and trust, the boundary relation between these two spheres can seem frictionless, and structural differentiation can appear to produce integration and individuation. It must be clear to all but the most diehard free marketeers, however, that an industrializing, market economy also throws roadblocks in the way of civil society. In the everyday language of social science, these blockages are expressed purely in terms of *economic* inequalities such as class divisions, housing differentials, dual labor markets, poverty, and unemployment. These economic facts can become crystallized as destructive intrusions into the civil realm, as economic criteria interfering with civil ones.

The stratification of economic products, both human and material, narrows and polarizes civil society. It provides a broad field for the discourse of repression, which pollutes and degrades economic failure. Despite the fact that there is no inherent relationship between failure to achieve distinction in the economic realm and failure to sustain expectations in civil society, such a connection is continually made. If you are poor, you are often thought to be irrational, dependent, and lazy, not only in the economy but in society as such. The relative asymmetry of resources inherent in economic life, in other words, becomes translated into projections about civil competence and incompetence. It is often difficult for actors without economic achievement or wealth to communicate effectively in the civil sphere, to receive full respect from its regulatory institutions, or to interact with other, more economically successful people in a fully civil way. Finally, material power as such, power garnered only in the economic realm, too often becomes an immediate and effective basis for civil claims. Despite the fact that the professionalization of journalism has separated ownership and effective control, capitalists can buy, sell, and shut down newspapers, communicative institutions central to civil society, thus fundamentally altering the cultural construction of the civil scene.

Yet, to the degree that civil society exists as an independent force, economically underprivileged actors have dual memberships. They are not only unsuccessful members of the economy; they also have the ability to make claims for respect and power on the basis of their only partially realized membership in the civil realm. On the basis of the implied universalism of civil solidarity, moreover, they believe these claims should find a response. They make use of the communicative institutions of civil society, of social movements that demand socialism (or simply economic justice), and of voluntary organizations (such as trade unions) that demand fairness to wage employees. Sometimes they employ their space in civil society to confront economic institutions and elites directly, winning concessions in face-to-face negotiations. At other times, they make use of regulatory institutions, like law and the franchise, to force the state to intervene on their behalf in economic life. While these efforts at repair often fail, often they do succeed in institutionalizing workers' rights. Civil criteria now enter directly into the economic sphere. Dangerous working conditions are prohibited; discrimination in labor markets is outlawed; arbitrary economic authority is curtailed; unemployment is controlled and humanized; wealth itself can be redistributed according to criteria antithetical to those of a strictly economic kind.

The functional forces of these non-civil spheres have also fundamentally undermined civil society in different times and different ways, especially as they have become intertwined with segmentations created by time and space. In Catholic countries, Jews and Protestants have often been construed as uncivil and prevented from fully entering civil life. For most of the history of civil societies, patriarchal power in the family has translated into a lack of civil status for women. Scientific and professional power have empowered experts and excluded ordinary persons from full participation in vital civil discussions. Political oligarchies, whether in private organizations or in national governments themselves, have used secrecy and manipulation to deprive members of civil society from access to information about crucial decisions that affect their collective life.

In the course of Western history, these intrusions have been so destructive that the social movements organized for repair, and the theorists who articulate their demands, have often come to believe that such blockages are intrinsic to civil society itself. Socialists have argued that civil society is essentially and irrevocably bourgeois, that as long as there are markets and private property in the economic realm, people can never be treated in respectful and egalitarian ways. Radical feminists have argued that civil societies are inherently patriarchal, that the very idea of a civil society is impossible to realize in a society that has families which allow men to dominate women. Zionists argue that Western societies are fundamentally anti-Semitic. Black nationalists have claimed that racism is essential, and that the civil realm in white settler societies will always and necessarily exclude blacks.

138

In response to such arguments, radical intellectuals, and many of their followers as well, have chosen to exit rather than exercise voice. They have demanded the construction of an entirely different kind of society, one in which the uncivil nature of the spheres that border civil society would be fundamentally changed. Sometimes these revolutionary demands, and the reactionary efforts to undercut them, have destroyed civil societies. To the degree that national regimes have institutionalized some genuine autonomy for their realms, however, these critics have succeeded not in making revolutions but in creating dramatic reforms. Revolutionary efforts have usually failed, but the claims they lodge have often succeeded in expanding civil society in significant ways. The result, rather than exit, has been the incremental but real integration of formerly excluded groups. Inclusion is never complete, but it has been substantial.

To the degree that there is institutionalization of a civil sphere, economic, political, and religious problems are not treated merely – or sometimes even primarily – as problems within these spheres themselves but as problems of "society." They are treated, both by those making claims and by those on the receiving end, as deficits in civil society itself, as forces that threaten society's cohesiveness, integrity, morality, and liberty. This is particularly the case because the functional stratification of civil society often merges with the stratification caused by the instantiation of civil society in time and space. Functional problems become intertwined with primordial questions about the capacities generated by race, language, region, timing of arrival, and loyalty to the nation itself. This intertwining makes it even more likely that each of these different kinds of conflicts – functional, spatial, and temporal – will be seen not incidentally but primarily as demands for inclusion into the civil sphere. In this situation, inclusion becomes an end in itself, not merely a means of particular repair. Conflicts become struggles for identity and social recognition, for repairing the fragmentation and distortion of civil society itself.

— 8 —

PSYCHOTHERAPY AS CENTRAL INSTITUTION

As emotional practice and as intellectual frame, psychotherapy has become a central feature of modern life. As the travails of the subjective self have become a pivotal reference to our time, psychotherapy has become a major institution. Therapeutic practice focuses on a single self in a private space, but this does not mean it is not social. Psychotherapy is as central to modernity as the school, the hospital, the confessional, the bureaucracy, the market, and the jail. That it has gone largely unmentioned in social theory suggests we have ignored one of the central avenues for "repairing" the dark side of modernity in contemporary life.

Subjectivity and self have been central to the ideas and practices of modernity in both their rationalist and romantic lines. From the contract theories of Locke and Rawls to the Enlightenment ideas of Kant and Habermas, rationalist philosophers have not ignored the self, but have stressed its capacity for self-consciousness, lucidity, calculation, balance, control, and objectivity. These emphases complement scientific thought, whose confidence in the inner rationality of the self has had the effect of shifting the focus of modern society to the outward rather than the inner world, to things rather than to consciousness. According to the twin preoccupations of rationalism and materialism, the science of nature can unlock the doors not only of health but happiness, overcoming disease and economic want. A new science of the brain can explain emotions and produce medications to control them. The materialist culture of capitalist society has undoubtedly contributed much to this. In a world surfeited by ever changing, ever more clever and attractive things, it seems natural to look outward rather than inward, to emphasize quantity over quality, the conquest of space and time rather than inner meaning and consciousness.

Yet, this objective line of modernity has never been hegemonic. If it were, how could we understand the lineage of criticism, from Blake to Huxley, from Fukuyama to Hollebeck? Objective modernity has been doubled by subjective modernity. The development and unfolding of an inner life, in all its irrationality, has from the beginning constituted a parallel modern universe. Those who have explored the poetry and theory of inner life, and developed its counter-practices, have despised rationalism and its objectifying results.

The countermovement begins with romanticism, with Blake's passionate attacks on "dark satanic mills" and Wordsworth's turning inward to light "the lamp of experience," with the violent rejection of classicism in the music of Beethoven, the philosophy of John Ruskin, and the paintings of Turner and Friedrichs. There emerged a romantic religion, the pietistic and evangelical movements that offered anti-ascetic practices and theories of salvation from the middle of the eighteenth century. In social thought, the countermovement begins with Hegel, on the one side, and Emerson and the American transcendentalists on the other. Later, we can trace the rebellion of John Stuart Mill against his father's utilitarianism, the son's searching for emotional life in romantic love. We can trace the movement against Kantianism in Nietzsche's insistence on rituals in life and art, in the philosophies of Dilthey and Bergson which emphasized identity, inner meaning, and emotional particularity, and in Durkheim's and Tarde's sociologies of non-irrational symbolic communication and effervescent emotional energy.

The new systematic thinking about subjectivity and consciousness that marked the early years of the twentieth century (see chapter 1) represented less a breakthrough than a series of further developments along these lines. Husserl revealed the hidden irrationality of objective cognition, and promoted phenomenological reduction as a method for shutting out external reality so as to highlight subjective perception. Heidegger, full of hatred for the technology of modernity, fled from epistemology to ontology, from rational existence to the being that supposedly underlay it. Language philosophy turned from objective reference to subjective representation, rooting language not in practicality but in subjective conventions and mental systems. An incurable romantic, Wittgenstein feared modernity and his life was marked by sometimes tragic efforts to escape it. For the most creative twentieth-century Marxism, the enemy was not poverty or exploitation but materialism and reification, a principal manifestation of which was modern scientific rationality.

The dramatic transformations in twentieth-century literature and painting followed similar lines. From post-impressionism to cubism, surrealism, abstract expressionism, color field painting, and minimalism, we observe the movement away from objective reflection and towards the blurred and symbolic representation of inner life. Henry James turned away from action and events to explore the non-linear and associational pathways of inner consciousness. Proust withdrew from the world and reconstructed icons of memory. Joyce destroyed the linearity of time and the logic of inner thinking. Virginia Woolf developed a new way of writing to represent the anti-realism of thinking and feeling.

The social and cultural forces that created such artistic and intellectual developments gave birth to a new "science" of mental and emotional life. Psychoanalysis made its public appearance on the first day of the twentieth century, when Sigmund Freud published *The Interpretation of Dreams*. Insisting on the subjective origins of action and institutions, Freud suggested that moderns should stop asking, "Why do bad things happen to me," and ask instead, "What have I done to create these bad things?" Internal psychical process creates the sense of exterior compulsion. It is the movement from subject to object – the "projection" of attitudes onto others that are in reality one's own – that creates the seeming externality and other-orientation of the world. So the psychotherapeutic parallels the phenomenological reduction. Patient and therapist must assume, for the sake of argument as well as for the purposes of self-change, that the self alone is responsible for the actor's social world.

142

This presupposition triggers the basic questions of psychotherapy. The first question is, Who am I? The answer to this question has led millions of persons away from the rational and outward-looking tenets of the objective line in modern life. To find out who I am is to leap into the inner and invisible world of illogic, subjectivity, and fragmented experience. By practicing therapy and reading Freud, modern persons have discovered they are guided less by discipline and common sense than by desires and deceptions, by fears and infantile illusions. They have not fully grown up, but remain childlike in an adult world, hoping as much for dependence as for autonomy.

The second question psychoanalysis asks is, How did I become this way? The answer it offers is that people become themselves because of their object relations. These are not the external objects of the material world encountered by rational human beings. They are, rather, the human objects encountered by vulnerable and half-formed children, when they are not able to distinguish truth from reality, as Sartre so vividly suggested in the opening of *Les Mots*. Such objects are not understood rationally and dealt with effectively, in a modern and pragmatic way. Rather, they are "cathected," connected to emotionally, and brought, in distorted versions, from outside to inside one's self. From early childhood, the actor is formed from these internalized objects, whose relations create dynamics inside the self.

It is to the reconstruction of these objects that psychotherapy is directed. The idea is to develop a fuller and more independent self, to lift the repressive force attached to internalized early objects and the irrational anxiety they inspire, and thus to prevent the compulsive repetition of self-destructive behavior. Therapy allows the modern actor to rearrange these internal objects. After such inner transformation, better relationships can be formed with the external world. The practice of psychotherapy is not about action and the alteration of time and space. Such modern operations are suspended. Objects are explored not through distant and neutral study but through free association and inner experience. Nothing happens in psychotherapy. There is only insight.

No sophisticated Western person in the twentieth century could fail to be aware of such Freudian truths. They deeply affected the

143

cultural and social sciences, and every form of aesthetic creativity from painting to poetry, from novels to film. Of what other among the new subjective philosophies that emerged in the twentieth century can this be said?

An austere ideational system that so powerfully permeates social thinking and representation has already become a practical philosophy. But psychoanalysis became even more "social" than this. Its understanding of the self gave birth to a new form of social practice, a thing called psychotherapy undertaken by tens of millions of people. This new practice addressed an invisible sickness, internal diseases of mental illness and neurosis. What had earlier been a sickness of the soul, diagnosed by priests and addressed by dogma and ritual ablution, became an emotional disease, treated in a one-to-one relationship focused on the inner life, the goal of which was to teach the self how to be more free.

Being "in therapy" became a common experience in everyday life, being a therapist became a widely accepted career. There are schools and disciplines, examinations and licenses, salaries, insurance companies, conferences and professional hierarchies – all the trappings of modern professions. Today, at the beginning of the twenty-first century, depression, anxiety, and eating disorders are considered major illnesses. At any one time, some 25 percent of elite American college students take psychiatric medications, even as the queues for publicly insured "talking therapy" are extended and private practices fill up. On November 30, 2005, in a lead article in the *Guardian*, bold headlines announced: "Therapy for all who need it on the NHS [National Health Service]. A network of the counseling centers for the depressed and anxious. Could the government be about to take mental health seriously?" (O'Hara 2005). The report's opening lines illustrate the institutional centrality of psychoanalytic theory and practice at the beginning of the new century:

> Lying across the path of productive happiness, goes the theory, stands mental illness, the common afflictions of depression and anxiety. Our society may be more affluent than ever before, but never has it been less at ease with itself.
>
> In the next few weeks, the government is expected to announce plans aimed at transforming the mental wellbeing of millions of people across

Britain. The Department of Health is expected to back recommenda-
tions . . . advocating the widespread introduction of psychological treatments – the so-called "talking therapies" – in the NHS for the estimated
5 million people in Britain with non-acute mental health conditions.

Reporting on government plans for recruiting 10,000 new NHS
therapists and creating a network of 250 independent therapy
treatment centers, the *Guardian* calls it "a ringing endorsement of
what some critics dismiss as a 'therapy culture,' " i.e. "the notion
that individual and societal ills can be solved by talking things
through with a counselor."

Therapy culture became less strictly psychoanalytic as it adapted
itself to different institutional domains in modern life. In the
United States, there is now short-term employment counseling
provided by most major companies and public institutions.
Churches supply pastoral care, and some support Christian psychotherapy. Twelve step programs, which began with Alcoholics
Anonymous, have developed for every form of addiction from
eating to sex to overspending. There are self-actualization movements and self-help books instructing readers how to get in touch
with the inner self. There are therapy call-in radio shows and
therapy-like encounters organized by television talk show hosts
about ruinous childhoods and inner pain.

In all these different manifestations, the philosophy is much the
same. The instruction is to turn away from external things and
authorities and to move inward toward the self, to recognize and
take on board the irrational and regressive impulses and beliefs
that threaten to engulf the self. It is about providing an experience
of private life, of protecting it from the intrusions of the public
sphere, of nurturing the self so it can experience fuller and more
balanced emotions and become healthy enough, not only to participate in modern disciplines, but to sustain love and friendship.
None of this can be done by the community or the state, by money
or social movement. Social subjectivity must be nurtured in private
spaces that allow individuals to experience themselves and others
in an emotional relationship of confrontation, dialogue, and
respect.

It would be surprising if such a novel yet deeply institutionalized
idea and practice did not inform the new social movements that

145

emerged in the later twentieth century. The 1960s New Left was characterized by a sharp shift away from materialism to more subjective concerns with fulfillment and authenticity, with ending repression and expressing real feelings, its most original theorist, Herbert Marcuse, moving from traditional Marxism to radical Freudian theory. The American women's movement that emerged in the late 1960s and early 1970s developed from "consciousness raising" sessions that often took on psycho-dramatic forms. Gay rights movements demanded the right to express "who I really am." It seems likely, indeed, that not only the practice but the very conception of identity politics grew out of psychoanalytic thinking about how needs for recognition and selfhood created periodic developmental crises over identity.

There is no doubt that psychotherapy represents a knowledge and practice that reflects Western liberal thought. It is about negative liberty, about voluntarism and privacy, not about what can and must be done through public life or the positive freedoms that can be provided only by states. Yet describing this emotional theory and practice as liberal should not suggest its relevance is limited to the West. When the dust cleared after the Cultural Revolution in China, Chinese physicians began to reach out to Western institutions for psychoanalytic training. When European and Americans practiced in China, they reported their patients' symptoms were familiar. There were complaints about anxiety and isolation, about feelings of guilt and remorse. As their society changed and modernized, Chinese patients, too, needed to find ways to experience their subjective selves. Modernity cannot survive in a purely objective and rational form. It needs romance, a connection to the inner life. Modernity must be connected to subjectivity if the modern self is to be repaired and thrive.

— 9 —

THE FRICTIONS OF MODERNITY AND THEIR POSSIBLE REPAIR

Classical and modern thinkers like Marx, Weber, Durkheim, Simmel, Parsons, and Eisenstadt theorized a transition from early societies to modern ones. Societies would shift over time from kin-networked, aristocratic, village centered, agricultural, decentralized, magical, and theological orders to more depersonalized and centralized industrial orders, organized around large cities and nation-states, as science-based and rationally planned as human folly would allow them to be.

This "great transition" (Polanyi 1957) would unfold over centuries and even millennia, and it would not necessarily have to be linear. It would always be a matter, to employ Trotsky's term, of uneven and combined development, with such semi-modern patrimonial empires as China and India emerging long before early modern Europe. Some regions and spheres would be modernizing, while others would remain, for a time, rooted in more traditional culture and social organization. There would also be "artificial" sources of leads and lags. Five centuries of Western imperialism, for example, prevented many of the world's regions, cultures, and civilizations from completing transitions to modernity. Western modernity tried to supplant these other pathways. After imperialism was finally defeated in the early and middle twentieth century, transitions to modernity have resumed their multiple forms (Eisenstadt 2003).

Given the uneven path of development, it was acknowledged, there might be major adjustments along the way – like overthrowing capitalism, which Marx viewed as a barbarism preventing the modern transition from being completed. Still, whether equated with democratic capitalism, social democracy, or communism, the benefits of modernity were bound eventually to become available. Once this happened, nothing much would be changed. Modernity was conceived as an end point, the *telos* of a transition that allowed rationality, or at least rationalization; equality, or at least differentiation; freedom, or at least autonomy vis-à-vis the powers that be. Above all, modernity would allow flexibility, the ability to continuously process information and adapt action to the environment.

Things did not turn out this way. Even before modern social theory was created, it had already become evident that modernity was Janus-faced, not only progressive, benevolent, and competent, but primitive, malevolent, and irrational. It produced, not merely troubling, but deeply dangerous strains. Slavery and racial domination were fundamental to Western modernity; so was the "orientalist" prejudice toward Eastern civilizations that fostered feelings of superiority and contempt (Said 1978; Steinmetz 2007). These particularistic ethnic and racial ideas were rarely conceptualized by classical and modern theory. Neither were modern religious animosities. Virulent anti-Semitism was rarely acknowledged, and then only as a residue of "primordialism" left over from pre-modern, traditional times. With education, and further social development, modernity would self-correct. The great thinkers were likewise insensitive to what Claude Lévi-Strauss (1974 [1955]) called the original sin of modernity. East, West, North and South, modernity had obliterated the social and cultural systems of the world's first peoples and, indeed, the vast majority of aboriginal individuals themselves.

Such dark forces fuelled modernity long before the twentieth century, the dawning of which brought high hopes that the final stages of the transition would be completed (chapter 2, above). In that century, now barely behind us, science did flourish; industrial and then post-industrial economies did create staggering increases in productivity; socialism and communism did frequently push capitalism aside; large cities did displace rural society; non-Western nation-states were finally freed from empires and began to govern their own affairs; and efforts at rational "plannification" everywhere thrived.

Contrary to the predictions of most modern thinkers, however, the results of such changes were often horrific, sometimes threatening the very existence of human societies. Racism flourished after slavery had been abolished. Anti-Semitism accelerated after the Jews were emancipated. National chauvinism blossomed after the break-up of empires. Science created weapons of mass destruction. Planning led to unintended irrationalities, encouraged surveillance, and often displaced beauty with banality. Capitalist democracies created vast inequalities and often increased immiseration. Socialism stifled economic innovation, communism created dictatorship. In the last century of modernity, bloody revolutions were rife. On the right, they led to racist oppression and total war; on the left, they triggered new forms of repression, violence, and widespread material suffering. The twentieth century invented two new forms of social evil – totalitarianism and genocide.

If the great social thinkers failed to provide tools for explaining these grave shortcomings of modernity, neither could they explain why twentieth-century societies sometimes got it right. How did imperialism end? How were wars opposed and sometimes prevented? How were racism, anti-Semitism, and sexism sometimes attacked and often destroyed? How were totalitarian dictatorships overthrown, and why?

Because of the inadequacies of modern theory, in the late twentieth century postmodern challenges to classical and modern social theories emerged. Foucault (1980) addressed major deficits, and so have the theories about gender, race, sex, and disability that followed in his wake. But the binarism of postmodern theory is ahistorical; its understanding of cultural process too thin; its institutional ideas insufficiently undeveloped. It throws the modernist baby out with the bathwater.

The message of this book has been that contemporary social theory must absorb the lessons of failed modernity in order to conceptualize not only its light but its dark side. While frontally addressing the dangerous frictions at the core of contemporary life, theory needs also to eschew the apocalyptic sensibility that often undermines critical theory. Social theorists of the great transitions were right about one thing. Modernity can allow flexibility and adaptation. Perverse social arrangements can be monitored, occasionally prevented, and sometimes repaired. There are self-correcting capacities inside modernity that sometimes allow contemporary societies to get it right.

Strain 1: Hierarchy-bureaucracy-secrecy

Endemic social forces create hierarchies inside social organization, and sociologists have offered powerful explanation of why they often become impersonal and bureaucratic and why secrecy and elitism persistently result. When this unholy trinity defines the nation-state, there is authoritarianism and dictatorship. Even in formal democracies, the tendency to oligarchy remains relentless (Michels 1961 [1911]), distorting the organization of corporations, state agencies, universities, professions, voluntary organizations, and churches.

Possible repair

(a) *Social movements.* Throughout the history of modernity, critical, self-generating, and organized mass movements have periodically challenged institutional authorities. They are fundamental to any plausible theoretical understanding of the contemporary world (Touraine 1992).

(b) *Constitutions.* The rule of law – from judge-made to constitutional – has often provided critical leverage against hierarchy and secrecy (Dworkin 1977).

(c) *Mass media.* Journalism challenges hierarchy when news reporting is organized horizontally, as an internally regulated profession; when news reporting and editing is independent of direct corporate and state control, ethically committed to balance and objectivity, and written for a broad public audience (Schudson 2008).

(d) *Social criticism.* Modernity creates not only obedience but a culture of critical discourse (Gouldner 1979). In most modern societies, criticism becomes an influential profession. Independent reviewers exercise outsized influence, from adjudicating success in the arts to evaluating consumer goods and services. Criticism is also institutionalized in intellectual magazines, editorial departments of newspapers, blogs, and universities (Roberge 2011, 2012).

(e) *Demands for transparency.* Modernity can encourage a populist suspicion of secrecy. Public opinion frequently demands that authorities publicly justify their decisions (Habermas 1984). Freedom of Information laws have recently allowed civil society organizations to force the release of state secrets. A new social role of "whistleblower" has emerged to designate organizational insiders who "go public" with information that higher-ups keep secret, and laws have often been passed to protect them.

Strain 2: Commodification

The logic of capitalist markets can be chaotic, impersonal, and destructive. Concentrating on exchange value detaches economic actors from other kinds of social concerns, allowing them to be innovative and ruthlessly efficient. But calculating profit also has negative repercussions, from encouraging exploitation to downsizing that leaves millions out of work, to the emptying out of communities and regions that creates vast and destabilizing internal migrations. Commodification also produces ever more esoteric forms of financialization, the economic effects of which often surpass the capacity of capitalists themselves to understand. Such technologies for financial commodification as "mortgage derivatives" have created panic, suffering, and new inequalities throughout the global capitalist order today.

Possible repair

From the beginning of modern capitalism, decommodification (Kopytoff 1986) has challenged the abstract logic of market exchange.

(a) *Regulation.* Governments have engaged in continual struggles to regulate capitalist markets, not only for the protection of non-economic society (Polanyi 1957) but to maintain the wealth-producing capacities of capitalism itself. Examples range from central banks to safety rules, from rights for labor to organized deposit insurance.

(b) *The consumer revolution.* Consumption represents another, more counter-intuitive pathway of decommodification. It removes goods from the marketplace and places them inside the emotional domain of subjective private life. From the bourgeois consumer revolution in eighteenth-century Europe (Campbell 1987) to mass consumption among the middle, working, and even under-classes today, consumption allows individuation and moral regulation (Miller 1998), and creates opportunities for hedonistic pleasure and aesthetic styling (Campbell 1987).

Strain 3: The culture industry

According to critical theorists, commodification converts culture into an industry (Horkheimer and Adorno 1969). It replaces art with mechanical reproduction (Benjamin 1968 [1936]), reduces popular culture to kitsch, and creates mind-numbing uniformity via mass culture and advertisement.

Possible repair

(a) *The avant-garde.* Despite this prediction, high culture has thrived under capitalism. The modern avant-garde, itself often outspokenly anti-capitalist, introduces continuously unpredictable and often disturbing aesthetic innovations. Some of these creative efforts are powerfully rewarded in vigorous art markets for new music, painting, architecture, and sculpture.

(b) *Popular culture.* From photography and sound recording to radio, film, television, and digital reproduction, new forms of mechanical production have created rich possibilities for symbolically working through collective emotion. In the process, they have themselves become increasingly complex aesthetic vehicles, frequently providing new media for the practice of high art.

Strain 4: Isolation

Modernity broke down traditional communities, stretching the boundaries of collective organization over widening physical distances. Critics argue this produces increasing isolation, drawing a dystopian portrait of a society lacking social ties.

Possible repair

While physical extension of modernity is certainly real, each stretching of distance has stimulated technological inventions that allow interpersonal communication to be sustained over greater distance as well. First came the railroad, then the telegraph, and in short order, the telephone, automobile, airplane, fax, internet, mobile communication devices, social media, and such global face-to-face communication devices as Skype.

Strain 5: Othering

While classical and modern theorists conceptualized rationalistic and abstract forms of domination such as class and bureaucracy, they rarely theorized hierarchies based on concrete cultural difference, dominations formed around gender, sex, race, ethnicity, religion, and region (Seidman 2013).

Possible repair

Exclusion based on difference has been challenged, and sometimes counterbalanced, by incorporative processes (Alexander 2006) that allow persons to get out from under stigmatized identities and enter into the mainstream of social life. In the assimilative mode of incorporation, difference remains stigmatized, and individuals are encouraged to normalize by adopting the qualities of the dominant culture. More multicultural modes of incorporation challenge such homogenizing conformity. Groups can demand recognition of their cultural difference, denying the facile equation of civil capacity with fidelity to dominant values. Multiculturalism has emerged as an alternative mode of incorporation not only inside nation-states in the emerging global civil sphere. As early as the nineteenth century, the Western avant-garde embraced key elements of Japanese and Chinese aesthetics, and its later incorporation of African sculpture profoundly transformed modern Western painting and sculpture. Today, broad movements of cultural cross-pollination travel back and forth between East, West, North, and South, and not only in the aesthetic domain. One noted scholar has recently devoted a lengthy book to "the Easternization of the West" (Campbell 2007).

Strain 6: Nationalism

Predatory nationalism continues to rage in every region of the world, and it remains one of the tragic ironies of modernity.

Possible repair

In the second half of the twentieth century, unprecedented forms of transnational cooperation have emerged, such as the European Union. There have also been new levels of communicative globalization, including such phenomena as cheap air travel, mass tourism, world music, and global pop culture. International human rights law has also advanced.

Strain 7: War

There has not been hot global war since 1945, and proxy warfare between global powers disappeared with the fall of the Soviet Union 25 years ago. Yet, hugely destructive military conflicts continue, waged by states and non-state forces alike. Research and production of cutting-edge military technology remains competitive and intense.

Possible repair

New cultural and institutional techniques for preventing war were created over the course of the twentieth century. In the wake of that century's major conflicts, for example, complex "trauma processes" emerged (Alexander 2012). They created symbolic and emotional pathways for perpetrators to make apologies and reparations (Giesen 2004), for reconciliation and broader solidarity, and for some forms of post-national global organization. Postwar West Germany and the European Union represent paradigmatic examples of possibilities for postwar repair at the regional level. "Truth and Reconciliation Commissions," which first emerged in post-Apartheid South Africa (Goodman 2010), represent such possibilities at the national level, with the potential for tamping down the vicious cycle of revenge and violence that can follow upon civil war.

Strain 8: Techno-scientific destruction

Objective knowledge about nature has driven technological advances throughout modernity. Yet, these developments have been shadowed, if not overshadowed, by techno-scientific forces of mass destruction that have fuelled wars and created environmental desecration, from nuclear bombs to the poisoning of water and land, and global warming.

Possible repair

Modernity has spawned world-wide countermovements from anti-nuke campaigns to environmentalism (Gibson 2009). These movements of repair themselves often depend on science and technology. Geothermal and climate science discovered global warming, and satellite technology allows monitoring of illegal nuclear proliferation.

Strain 9: Threats to the self

Classical and modern theorists rarely conceptualized the self, assuming it to be ascetic, outward looking, and disciplined for hard work. Yet, the modern self has also betrayed a remarkable fragility. Faced with the strains of modernity, emotional coherence and stability have often proven difficult to maintain, with grave effects not just for individuals but for societies.

Possible repair

Since Freud first conceptualized the emotionally complex self more than a century ago, psychotherapy has become a central institution of modernity (chapter 8, above), with spin-offs like "twelve-step programs" creating emotional technologies to address everything from addiction, anger, and overeating to over-spending and over-sexing. Public financing of such psychiatric treatments – "mental health parity" – is becoming a new entitlement. Trauma counseling is routinely provided to victims of drunk driving (Schmidt, 2014), rape, natural disaster, and mass murder, and a wide range of other new professions has emerged to minister to the modern self; from work counselors to marriage, family, sex, and couples therapists. "Spiritual" treatments that address the psyche through treatment of the body have become niche industries, such as aromatherapy, massage, yoga, fitness, nutrition, and meditation.

The emergence of what the late Foucault (1993) called "self-cultivation" has accompanied the stretching of the life cycle into ever more discrete phases. As a result, individual development has come to be increasingly characterized by "crises of transition." Until early in the twentieth century, the life course consisted of infancy, childhood, and adulthood. Adolescence (Fass 1979) and the identity crisis (Erikson 1950) appeared only in the early and mid-century; "youth" in the 1960s (Keniston 1965); the "midlife crisis" in the 1970s (Levinson 1978); "emerging adulthood" in the 1990s (Arnett 2004). Since then, old age, renamed as "maturity," has become subdivided into early, middle, and late. Moving from one stage to another has come to be characterized as a series of "passages" (Sheehy 1974), demanding heightened levels of introspection and self-control.

In this concluding chapter, I have challenged the idea that modernity is an antidote to the problems of traditional life, an endpoint in the process of social change. The bloody history of the twentieth century falsified this idea, and the dark side of modernity was already evident for centuries before. While identifying dangerous strains at the core of modern societies, however, I have also pointed to cultural and institutional forces that can ameliorate them. To focus only on the destructive side of modernity is misleading; modernity also produces capacities for self-repair. Whether contemporary societies will be able to make use of such capacities is another matter.

NOTES

1: SOCIAL THEORY BETWEEN PROGRESS AND APOCALYPSE

1 For the notion of "transformative capacity" as the rationalizing contribution of the Protestant Reformation, see Eisenstadt (1968b). By emphasizing perfectionism and reason, I am adding to this approach a more culturally specific element of intellectual history, and will question below its evolutionary cast.

2 For the centrality of the millennialist ideas in modern revolutions and reform movements, see Walzer (1965) on the English Revolution; Tuveson (1968) and Bloch (1985) on the American Revolution; Miller (1965) on early national reform in America; Yeo (1981) on Chartism and primitive Christianity; and Hyams (1973) on the communist revolutions more generally.

3 At several points in his work, Weber suggested that, via the Enlightenment, the "charisma of reason" inherited Puritanism's this-worldly asceticism and became the embodiment of the world-mastering heritage of religious rationalization. For the connection of Puritanism to the first great manifestation of "reason," the scientific revolution, see Merton (1970 [1939]) and Tenbruk (1974).

The connection between religious rationalization and the contemporary ethos of modernity has been obscured by Weber's instrumental and materialistic theorizing about the industrial society. The Parsonian tradition provided an antidote to this, but its generally optimistic, often Pollyanna-ish, thinking about modernity made its contributions to theoretical reflection less important.

4 For the religious and eschatological underpinnings of Marx's work, see Löwith (1949); of Hegel's, see Taylor (1975). For Marxism as a this-worldly metaphysic, see Alexander (2010).

5 Indeed, participation in these mass socialist parties seemed to have provided tens of thousands of low- and middle-status people not only with a firm conviction of the imminence of the new society but with an experience of actual salvation in this world. See, for example, the autobiography of Julius Braunthal, the Austro-Hungarian socialist leader, which presents Braunthal's participation and expectations in unmistakably millennial terms:

It was a great day in my life when I went . . . to the Working-Class Youth Club to register . . . It meant for me the firm resolve to help bring about nothing less than the New Jerusalem on earth in my own lifetime . . . For me the fact that the world was constantly changing was beyond any question. My problem was whether or not the time for the "final change" in human society had come . . . From Marx's *Manifesto* and Friedrich Engels' *Anti-Dühring*, which were among the first Socialist classics I had read, I believed that humanity had now entered the final stage of its history. (Braunthal 1945: 39–40)

6 At first glance, it seems quite extraordinary that, in a century humbled by horrid violence, this turn toward violence in radical philosophy was little remarked upon and infrequently criticized. Thus, Sartre's *Critique of Dialectical Reason* (1976 [1968]) was taken by left thinkers (e.g. Poster 1979) as an argument for community – for the movement from serial to fused groups – rather than as an apologia for violence, which it was as well. Aron's *History and the Dialectic of Violence* (1975) is the only serious critique of this theme in Sartre's work, and it has been virtually ignored. Aron argues that Sartre's work became so politicized that theoretical and ideological confusions are fused – "the taste for Revolution and a lack of it for reform have become a philosophical truth" (Aron 1975: 185). He attacks the degeneration of reason and the ultimate dehumanization this position involves: "The strange alliance between Reason and violence, whereby the other – the conservative, the reformist, anyone who says 'no' to the revolutionary apocalypse – takes on the grim traits of the anti-man" (ibid.). "It is by means of the class struggle, by the antagonism of groups where everyone wishes the death of the other, that the dialectical movement, whose completion is marked by the advent of totalizing Truth, progresses" (ibid.: 187–8).

In regard to the link between Fanon (1965) and Sartre, Aron is critical not of anticolonial violence as a strategic necessity but of its theoretical justification in antirational terms. "What I hate," he writes (ibid.: 192), "is not the choice, *hic et nun*, at a particular conjunction of circumstances, in favour of violence and against negotiation, but a philosophy of violence in and for itself, not as a means that is sometimes necessary for a rational politics, but a philosophy that lays claim to an ontological foundation and psychological function or effectiveness." The intellectual promotion of violence, of course, is hardly limited to the left. Highly respected geopolitical thinkers, such as Kissinger, have advocated the strategic use of massive deadly force (see Gibson 1986).

7 This is not an anachronistic usage, as Lenin's famous pamphlet *Left-Wing Communism: An Infantile Disorder* demonstrates.

8 "The notion that social change can be best achieved through revolutionary violence is very much an offshoot of the French Revolution and of its socialist heirs. Sorel's *Reflections sur la violence* took up an uncomfortable and hushed-up subject and made it the center of a strategy destined to overthrow the bourgeois order. At a time when the Marxists of the Second International were pussy-footing about the desirability of a revolution, Sorel took the uncompromising step of affirming its necessity" (Llobera 1988).

9 For a discussion of the historical dialectic between absent and present reason, see Alexander (1992c).

10 Once, it was only "anticommunists" who made such critical claims. More recent documentation of the communist distortion of reason came from newspapers within Soviet Russia itself. In spring 1988, in the wake of perestroika, the final history examinations of more than 50 million Soviet schoolchildren were canceled. In an extraordinary commentary on its front page, laced with expressions of bitterness, tortured guilt, and hopes for purification, *Izvestia* attacked the entire historiography of Soviet communism as the inversion of the Revolution's rational hopes. "The guilt of those who deluded one generation after another, poisoning their minds and souls with lies, is immeasurable. . . . Today we are reaping the bitter fruits of our own moral laxity. We are paying for succumbing to conformity and thus to giving silent approval of everything that now brings the blush of shame to our faces and about which we do not know how to answer our children honestly. [This process is] a purifying torture of revelation, or, to be precise, a second birth" (quoted in Parks 1988).

11 "[I]t is now the world of psychologically and morally exhausted societies (largely on a Marxist and post-Marxist pattern) that have lost their energy and appeal. They are seen, along with their philosophy, as antique fortresses jutting out of a wasteland of the past. In fact, their own chances of breaking out of this closure now depend largely on their success in following the new model set by America and its rivals and competitors in the Western imperium. . . . At the time of Nikita Krushchev's reform regime in the early 1960s, and again under Mikhail Gorbachev's drive in the mid-1980s to modernize the Soviet economy and partially open the society, there was discussion of a possible 'convergence' of the two adversary systems. But the pull of convergence was mostly one-sided, not toward the blocked societies of the East but toward the openness of the West." This polemical statement was remarkable not so much for what it said as for who said it – not a conservative Cold Warrior but the venerable New Deal liberal, Max Lerner (1987), in the liberal American magazine *The New Republic*.

12 "In the weeks before the Armageddon, Bethmann Hollweg's secretary and confident Kurt Riezler made notes of the gloomy relish with which his master steered Germany and Europe into the Abyss. July 7, 1914: 'The Chancellor expects that a war, whatever its outcome, will result in the uprooting of everything that exists. The existing world very antiquated, without ideas.' July 27: 'Doom greater than human power hanging over Europe and our people.' " (Johnson 1983: 12).

13 Lévi-Strauss begins *Tristes Tropiques* with an account of his encounter with "one of those outbreaks of stupidity, hatred, and credulousness which social groups secrete like pus when they begin to be short of space" (1974 [1955]: 18). He argues that "experiences such as these [are] starting to ooze out like some insidious leakage from contemporary mankind, which [has] become saturated with its own numbers and with the ever-increasing complexity of its problems" (ibid.). He concludes the book with this melancholic prophecy, not much different from the spirit of Wittgenstein's:

> The world began without man and will end without him. The institutions, morals and customs that I shall have spent my life noting down and trying to understand are the transient efflorescence of a creation in relation to which

160

they have no meaning . . . From the time when he first began to breathe and eat, up to the invention of atomic and thermonuclear devices, by way of the discovery of fire . . . what else has man done except blithely break down billions of structures and reduce them to a state in which they are no longer capable of integration? (ibid.: 472)

14 In his sociological explanation for the rise of existentialism in the years immediately after French liberation in 1944, Baert (2011) sees Sartre's philosophical notion of responsibility as providing an intellectual response to the trauma of French collaboration with Nazi occupation.

2: AUTONOMY AND DOMINATION: WEBER'S CAGE

1 This point is made decisively in the important essay by Seidman (1983b), which insists that Weber does not view the post-cosmological worlds in purely negative terms.
2 The only major exception is Löwith (1982), who differentiated Weber's rationalization theory from Marx's precisely in these terms; i.e., that Weber tied this development to the increased opportunities for existence in modern life. I take up this existential theme later in the chapter.
3 The darker side of rationalization has, of course, been pursued by Marxism, and the specifically Weberian understanding of this development has been elaborated within the Marxist tradition by "critical theory" (Habermas 1984). This tradition, however, has been unable to bring to its account of moral and social decline Weber's phenomenological thrust, particularly his commitment to understanding the role of independently constituted symbolic systems played in producing this darker side. The other traditions I have more in mind, therefore, are not Marxist ones but rather those of Elias and Foucault. Even these traditions, however, under-emphasize the power-mediating qualities of cultural texts.
4 This discussion of discipline demonstrates that there are fundamental connections between one tendency in Weber's sociology and the theory of modernity produced by Foucault (e.g., most directly, Foucault 1975). Yet, while Foucault certainly draws out the nature and ramifications of anti-individualistic discipline to an extent Weber might only have imagined, he does so in a manner Weber would not have entirely approved. Foucault focused only on one side of the dialectic of domination and individuality; he did not see that the expanding domination he described was intimately tied up with the extension of individuality. In the second place, Foucault insisted on a relatively recent "epistemological break" as the source of discipline, failing to develop a comparative understanding of this phenomenon that gives to Western discipline a much longer *durée*. At least in his disciplinary writings, Foucault is able to appreciate the continuing vitality of human responsibility in the modern world, much less its sociological foundations. The same can be said for many other contemporary cultural critics, for example MacIntyre (1981) and Bell (1976). See note 7, below.
5 Here my interpretation departs sharply from the "neo-religious" tack taken by Shils (1975) and other conservatives.

6 Mitzman (1970) is not the only interpreter to make the former charge, i.e. that Weber saw irrational, charismatic politics as the only way out. Loewenstein (1966) and Mommsen (1974), for example, have made much the same point. Parsons and Bendix are the major figures associated with the identification of Weber as a progressive liberal who saw freedom as the emerging product of world history. Though Schluchter's interpretation of Weber is more nuanced (1981), he too seriously underplayed the apocalyptic, darker side of Weber's work. Habermas (1984) extends these three liberal interpreters, though he is much more critical of Weber's failure to spell out the prerequisites even of a liberal and democratic society and more aware of the negative side of the dialectic. Habermas fails to illuminate this side of Weber's work fully because he conflates it with the anti-normative instrumentalism of critical theory (see Alexander 1985).

7 Ignoring the subtleties of Weber's argument, many contemporary social theorists describe the modern condition as a choice between chaotic freedom and conservative regulation. Thus, drawing on Weber, MacIntyre (1981) claims one must choose between Nietzsche and Aristotle, and he chooses the teleological, hierarchalized value-framework of the latter. Neo-conservatives like Bell (1976) pose a similar choice and reject the fragmentation of modernity for religious revival. In doing so, such theorists are succumbing to what I earlier called "metaphysical nostalgia," an intellectual form of world-flight.

8 See Levine (1981) for a strong argument that Weber failed to develop the kind of motivational theory that could account for such significant "rational" movements in modernity as psychotherapy. See also chapter 9.

3: BARBARISM AND MODERNITY: EISENSTADT'S REGRET

1 Parsons also took this "yes" from Durkheim, especially the first two books of *The Division of Labor in Society* (1984 [1893]). To mention Durkheim and his relationship to modernity is to suggest the self-imposed limitations of the present chapter. My ambition is to set the debate about modernity in the framework of the ambiguities of "rationalization" not only as fact but also as theory. This specific manner of framing the question of modernity has been enormously productive philosophically and sociologically, marking the German and German-influenced traditions most strongly, though it has emerged in other national traditions as well. Still, when American pragmatists like John Dewey spoke of rationalization, it was in a much different vein than the subjects of this chapter. American pragmatists typically were more positive and optimistic, even if equally critical of capitalism. While there is little doubt that Parsons draws from this American tradition in his liberal incorporation of Weber, I view his perspective on modernity as another systematic response to the rationalization theme (see chapter 4).

2 On the role that desire for transcendence played in radical right-wing ideology, see Nolte (1966).

3 A fuller treatment of the "no" reaction to modernity, for example, would have to explore the complexities of romanticism. The aesthetic, cognitive, and moral development of romanticism forms the key counterpoint to

rationalized modernity. Emerging in late eighteenth and early nineteenth-century literature, music, art, and philosophy – for one of the best general accounts of this movement, see, Abrams (1953) – romanticism did not necessarily take an antidemocratic or anti-Enlightenment form. As Steven Seidman pointed out in *Liberalism and the Origins of European Social Theory* (1983a), romanticism often opposed hyper-rationalization, while embracing rationality in a broader sense, via such themes as expressive individualism, authenticity, creativity, and reciprocity. For this broader argument, see Taylor (1989).

4 The most important recent study of the Axial Age and its radical de-centering of human history is Robert Bellah's *Religion in Human Evolution: From the Paleolithic to the Axial Age* (2011), which includes a sustained reflection on the breakthrough in China and India as well as in Israel and Greece.

5 These quintessentially modern feelings are captured by such terms as "ontological anxiety" – first employed, in a psychoanalytic version of existentialism, by R.D. Lang in *The Divided Self* (1966) and later by Giddens in *The Constitution of Society* (1984) – and "psychological man," which Philip Rieff developed in *The Triumph of the Therapeutic: Uses of Faith after Freud* (1968). The structural status of such anxieties explains why psychotherapy can make a claim to have been the most important and influential cultural invention of the twentieth century, and why so much contemporary popular literature is devoted to self-help guides for the perplexed and restless (see chapter 9).

6 Erich Fromm, *Escape from Freedom* (1941). Fromm's work should be seen as part of the dialogue about the dialectics of rationalization; he was a younger member of the Frankfurt school and a social analyst in the Freudian tradition.

7 For a penetrating study of militarism as a response to, and impression of, the rationalization of contemporary American life, see James William Gibson, *Warrior Dreams: Paramilitary Culture in Post-Vietnam America* (1994).

8 For this framing of the early American experience, see Edmund Morgan, *The Puritan Dilemma* (1958) and, most generally and powerfully, the works of Perry Miller, e.g., *Errand into the Wilderness* (1956), *Nature's Nation* (1967), and *The Life of the Mind in America* (1965). One of the great intellectual historians of American history, Miller's reflections about grace, salvation, social rationalization, and psychological release form an extraordinary counterpart to Weber's sociology. There has even emerged a "left-Millerism" that constructs violence less as a deviant than as a deeply institutionalized search for grace, e.g., Richard Slotkin, *Regeneration through Violence: The Mythology of the American Frontier, 1600–1860* (1973) and Gibson, *Warrior Dreams* (1994). Edward Tiryakian (1975) evoked this Miller tradition in American Studies in an imaginative effort to resolve the dilemmas of modernity articulated by classical sociology.

9 Both because of the American nation's Puritan-Protestant religious core, and because of the vast influence of Perry Miller's historical framing, the escape from this-worldly tension and the paths this escape have taken can be seen as a constant theme in the non-Marxist criticisms that American thinkers have leveled against themselves and their nation. See, e.g., David Riesman,

The Lonely Crowd (1950), Conrad Cherry, *God's New Israel* (1970), Philip Slater, *The Pursuit of Loneliness: American Culture at the Breaking Point* (1970), Robert N. Bellah, *The Broken Covenant: American Civil Religion in Time of Trial* (1975) and Bellah et al., *Habits of the Heart: Individualism and Commitment in American Life* (1985).

4: INTEGRATION AND JUSTICE: PARSONS' UTOPIA

1 Following Habermas's stress on the importance of Parsons' work, but more sympathetic and insightful about its sociological contribution to democratic social theory, Cohen and Arato (1995) make an intriguing connection between a critical civil society theory and Parsons' concept of influence. They argue that civil society, regulated by procedurally-oriented discourse ethics, grows out of the same preconditions that allow influence to replace money and power as the central medium of exchange. This discussion points to the democratic line in Parsons that I reference here, and levels some of the same criticisms I make below. The force of Cohen and Arato's argument is to some degree vitiated, however, by their insistence that the democratically appropriate form of influence can only be "the achievement of solidarity through discussion and deliberation of individuals who choose to participate in an association" (Cohen and Arato 1995: 131), a position they contrast with a conception of diffuse, value-based influence. From a sociological point of view, this distinction is untenable; discussions that are free and rational in a normative sense must be based on the presuppositions of a language game – a set of value commitments that is itself, at the time of argument, not open to question. That is a fundamental point of Parsons' analytical model of the generalized media of exchange, and it underscores the difference between empirical-sociological and normative-philosophical approaches to the civil sphere. Leon Mayhew (1997) presents a more institutionally-oriented critique of Parsons' societal community theory from a Habermasian perspective.

2 This critical reading differs fundamentally from Gerhardt's (2001) reconstruction.

> Parsons wrote the slim volume *Societies: Evolutionary and Comparative Perspectives* (1966). In the second chapter, the core of the book, he used the notion of societal community for the first time. He ventures what were the integrative forces that held a society together to the effect that social relations would not disintegrate in the face of institutional differentiation in the course of the history of modernization. His answer contained the concept of societal community, explained tentatively as that forum for moral commitment which rendered more or less diverse populations identifiable members united in their identification with their cultural and/or national common heritage. (Gerhardt 2001: 180)

3 Parsons hardly wrote about Stalinism, perhaps a legacy of his earlier 1930s "progressivism" and his liberal antagonism during the postwar period to the rigidly anti-communist foreign policy of American conservatives. When Parsons wrote about the USSR in the postwar period, he tended to emphasize

its modernizing tendencies and its capacities for evolutionary progress, implicitly opposing the more reactionary elements of America's Cold War foreign policy.

4 Sciortino (2001) presents an alternative to the critical reading I offer here, downplaying the conservative and nondemocratic lines of Parsons' societal community theory. Yet, even Sciortino notes Parsons' difficulty in articulating the "relational nexus between the normative definitions of membership . . . and the actual pattern of social solidarities and groupings existing in any given society," his "lack of a structural theory of solidary groups," and his focus in modern society on differentiation rather than on segmentary groups – "segmental categories are often mentioned but seldom placed at the center of inquiry."

5 This was exactly the point Mayhew (1968) made in the most acute criticism ever penned by a card-carrying Parsonian. Rather than seeing ascription – as Parsons did – as traditional and achievement as modern, Mayhew demonstrated how achievement carries strong functional imperatives that actually sustain ascription, such that ascription is often functionally efficient.

6 Cf. Cohen and Arato's (1995: 125) observation that Parsons' societal community theory "both elaborates the normative achievements of modernity and represents these as if they were already institutionalized," whereas the task of critical theory is to "throw much doubt on the claims of successful institutionalization."

5: DESPISING OTHERS: SIMMEL'S STRANGER

1 See, in this connection, Entrikin's (1991) epistemological critique of spatial arguments, in which he argues that abstract "spatial" position can be transformed into concrete social "place" only if it is subject to cultural narration.

2 "What makes certain people 'strangers' and therefore vexing, unnerving, off-putting and otherwise a 'problem', is their capacity to befog and eclipse the boundary lines . . . Mary Douglas taught us that what we perceive as uncleanness or dirt and busy ourselves scrubbing and wiping out is that anomaly or ambiguity 'which must not be included if the pattern is to be maintained' . . . The stranger is hateful and feared as is the slimy, and for the same reasons . . . The same relativity principle which rules the constitution of sliminess regulates the constitution of resented strangers" (Bauman 2001: 208–11).

3 For the argument that "movement intellectuals" define the meaning-structures that make social movements move, see Ron Eyerman and Andrew Jamison (1991).

4 For further studies, see, e.g., Smith (1991, 1998); Magnuson (1997); Alexander (1998b, 2003b, 2006, 2010); Edles (1998); Jacobs (2000).

5 The following quotations are from Said (1978: 37–9).

6 The following quotations, unless otherwise indicated, are from Kuisel (1993: 11–13).

7 The following quotations are drawn from the reproduction of the English version of this letter in Schaefer (1965: 37–9). The italics are mine.

6: MEANING EVIL

1 Against such an unreflective view, Geertz (1983) suggests that common sense be viewed as a cultural system – as an organizing symbolic structure that provides cognitive, moral, and emotional frameworks of interpretation. From this perspective, common sense is not a matter of pragmatics, a naturalistic reflection of some "real," everyday reality.

2 "As a moral concept, evil is an ancient and heavily freighted term . . . that sociology has defined itself against in the course of its development as an autonomous discipline . . . Sociology is characterized by a conscious distancing of itself from the term and a selective appropriation of ideas that fit the nascent discipline's idea of human nature and the positive telos of human evolution. Indeed, evil is sociology's doppelganger, always present, but unwelcome, haunting the discipline and its quest for Enlightenment by calling to mind questions of metaphysics, agency, and the 'dark side' of human progress" (Cushman 1998: 2–3).

3 "If the sacred is a projection of us *at our best*, and the world of the profane a representation of us *as we actually are*, including the manifestations of ordinary evil that we experience, radical evil can be conceptualized as a projection of us *at our worst*, the worst that we can prove to be while still maintaining those characteristics that make us – us as a community, a society, or humanity – what we are. In that sense evil, even radical evil, cannot be overcome. Concrete manifestations of it can be overcome – Auschwitz can be driven out of this world, ethnic cleansing hopefully can too – but if evil is a horizon that moves with us, then there will always be a collectively shared symbolic representation of what we, we as a single moral community or we as humans, can be at our worst. The idea of a good society where evil has been eradicated is, from a postmetaphysical standpoint, as meaningless as the idea of a pacified moral world where no conflict of value exists any longer" (Ferrara 2001).

4 "The values which come to be constitutive of the structure of a societal system are, then, the conceptions of the desirable type of society held by the members of the society of reference and applied to the particular society of which they are members . . . A value-pattern then defines a direction of choice, and consequent commitment to action" (Parsons 1968: 136).

Following Parsons, Robin M. Williams offered this authoritative sociological interpretation of American values: "A value system is an organized set of preferential rules for making selections, resolving conflicts, and coping with needs for social and psychological defenses of the choices made or proposed. Values steer anticipatory and goal-oriented behavior; they also 'justify' or 'explain' past conduct" (Williams 1971, especially p. 128).

5 Influenced by Bataille's emphasis on evil, Caillois (1959), rightly criticized Durkheim for not distinguishing clearly enough between the sacred, the profane, and the routine.

6 "It is inherent in our entire philosophic tradition that we cannot conceive of a 'radical evil' and this is true both for Christian theology, which conceded even the devil himself a celestial origin, as well as for Kant . . . Therefore we have nothing to fall back on in order to understand a phenomenon that nevertheless confronts us with its overpowering reality" (Arendt 1951).

166

Richard Bernstein shares this view. "The larger question looming in the background is whether our philosophic tradition – especially the modern philosophic tradition – is rich and deep enough to enable us to comprehend what we are asserting when we judge something to be evil" (Bernstein 2001: 56). After an exhaustive investigation of Kant's philosophic thinking, Bernstein's answer is "no."

7 In his reconstruction of the republican theory of virtue, Quentin Skinner (1978) emphasizes the role of altruistic cultural commitments.

8 Dewey's communicative-normative logic, so strikingly adumbrating Habermas's later theory, is perhaps most clearly articulated in Dewey's *Democracy and Education* (1966 [1916]). Because pragmatism has supplied social science with its theoretical resources for conceptualizing agency and selfhood, the enthusiastic equation of valuation – the act of valuing – with goodness has made it difficult to understand how social creativity and agency often contribute to evil.

> Sociological theorists of agency have, like sociological theorists in general, displaced evil. This displacement has much to do with the unbridled political optimism of the progenitors of the pragmatic theories of action [who] simply ignored the idea that the pragmatic, reflexive self could engage in action that was ferocious, malicious, and cruel in its genesis or outcome. Action and reflexivity was, for these thinkers and their later followers, always considered as progressive. This development was ironic, and perhaps even naïve, since such theories developed in a world historical context in which it was rather evident that agents used the infrastructure of modernity for nefarious rather than progressive ends. This belief in the optimistic and moral ends of agency is very clear [for example] in the work of Anthony Giddens, perhaps the most important contemporary theorist of agency. (Cushman 1998: 6)

> Discussions of agency . . . are celebratory and often heroic. According to one tradition, actors are rational, autonomous, self-sufficient, wily, and clever. According to another, they are knowledgeable, reflexive, self-monitoring, and routinely competent. In the rhetoric of a third approach, actors are endlessly creative, expressive, and meaning-making. [However,] if we do not conflate actors with agents, we are forced to recognize that actors are not nearly as heroic as these accounts imply. They are often befuddled, passive, self-deceptive, thoughtless, and vicious. How can this be so, if "agency" itself can be described in a positive way? The answer is that agency expresses itself only through its cultural and psychological environments, and these latter forces structure agency in open-ended and sometimes extraordinarily harmful ways. (Alexander 1992d: 4; see also Alexander 1998a)

9 While Bataille argues that "Good and Evil are complementary," he insists "there is no equivalence." He means to argue against moral relativism: "We are right to distinguish between behavior which has humane sense and behavior which has an odious sense. But the opposition between these forms of behavior is not that which theoretically opposes Good to Evil" (Bataille 1985 [1957]: 144).

10 Bernstein writes of this Kantian inability to conceptualize the sui generis autonomy of evil:

When we analyze what Kant means, the results are quite disappointing. Radical evil seems to be little more than a way of designating the tendency of human beings to disobey the moral law, not to do what they ought to do. There is a disparity between Kant's rhetoric – his references to "wickedness," "perversity," "corruption" – and the content of what he is saying . . . Kant's concept of an evil maxim is too limited and undifferentiated. The distinction between a good man and an evil man depends on whether or not he subordinates the "incentives of his sensuous nature" to the moral law as an incentive. (Bernstein 2001: 84)

The phrase "incentives of his sensuous nature" refers to the egoistic self who is not able to make a connection to values, which themselves are conceived inevitably as representations of the good.

11 While Foucault (and later postmodernist archeologists of modernity) found the production of evil, in the form of domination and pollution of the other, to be at the heart of modern thought and practice, he did not interpretively reconstruct "evil values" in the manner I am calling for here. Instead, he considered domination and pollution to be the product of power/knowledge – the rationalizing procedures of scientific rational knowledge and the "normalizing" social control accompanying it. In other words, Foucault followed the mainstream tradition in considering evil to follow, as an unintended consequence, from the (however misguided) normatively inspired effort to institutionalize the good. Foucault may have been influenced by the spirit of Bataille, but he did not follow the late Durkheimian roots of his thinking.

12 "According to Durkheim . . . we are not confronted with factually moral and factually immoral actions . . . Instead, it has been conceptually decided in advance that, essentially, there is only morality and solidarity, but that under certain regrettable circumstances these can be cut short from their full realization. Durkheim . . . conceives negation as mere deprivation, and to that extent his theory remains Aristotelian. Despite all his understanding for corruption and incompleteness, he expresses an affirmative attitude towards society" (Luhmann 1982: 9–10).

13 "The criterion for the radicality of radical evil ought perhaps to be internal to us, the moral community, rather than external, objective. Evil then is perhaps best conceived as a *horizon* that moves with us, rather than as something that stands over against us" (Ferrara 2001: 84).

14 This section is drawn from Alexander (1992a). I have subsequently elaborated this hermeneutic in a number of studies. It informs the cultural dimension of my 2006 book, *The Civil Sphere*.

15 The notion of the limit experience is the centerpiece of James Miller's investigation into what he views as the amoral, anti-humane life of Foucault, *The Passion of Michel Foucault* (1993), e.g. pp. 29, 398 n. 49. Without disputing Miller's moral judgment of Foucault's sexual behavior later in his life, which by several accounts evidenced a lack of concern for spreading HIV, I question Miller's effort to generalize from this accusation to a theoretical and philosophical indictment of Foucault's concentration on evil rather than on the good. Miller takes the notion of the limit experience as indicating a moral endorsement of the anti-morality of transgression. This is not the perspective of Bataille, nor should it be attributed to the theoretical perspective of Foucault.

16 For a discussion of Bataille's life and work, and the context of his time, see Richardson (1994) and Gill (1995). It has proven difficult to incorporate Bataille's thinking into streams of thought other than French-inspired post-modernist literary theory. While drawing fruitfully from the later, religious sociology of Durkheim and Mauss (see Pía Lara 2001: 208, n. 48), Bataille also tried, less fruitfully in my view, to develop a totalizing historical and existential philosophy, which included not only an ontology and a metaphysics but also a Marxist-inspired political economy. The short-lived "College de sociologie," which Bataille initiated with another third-generation Durkheimian Roger Caillois in the late 1930s, had a cultic and antinomian quality that aspired to the status of the Surrealist group of the World War I era. See Richman (1995) and Falasca-Zamponi (2011).

17 "To be 'bad' is to be mean in a precise sense of the term. Badasses manifest the transcendent superiority of their being, specifically by insisting on the dominance of their will, that 'I mean it,' when the 'it' itself is, in a way obvious to all, immaterial. They engage in violence not necessarily sadistically or 'for its own sake' but to back up their meaning without the limiting influence of utilitarian considerations or a concern for self-preservation. To make vivid sense of all the detailed ways of the badass, one must consider the essential project as transcending the modern moral injunction to adjust the public self sensitively to situationally contingent expectations" (Katz 1988: 81).

18 I draw here from "Human Rights Language in Amnesty International" (n.d.), section 4, pp. 24–5. I cannot locate the author of this very interesting manuscript, which, as far as I know, is as yet unpublished.

7: DE-CIVILIZING THE CIVIL SPHERE

1 This chapter draws from Alexander (2006, chapter 8).

BIBLIOGRAPHY

Abrams, M. H. (1953) *The Mirror and the Lamp: Romantic Theory and the Critical Tradition*. Oxford University Press, New York.

Aquinas, T. (2003) *On Evil*, trans. R. Regan. Oxford University Press, New York.

Alexander, J. C. (2012) *Trauma: A Social Theory*. Polity Press, Cambridge.

Alexander, J. C. (2010) Marxism and the Spirit of Socialism: Cultural Origins of Anti-Capitalism. *Thesis Eleven* 100, 84–105.

Alexander, J. C. (2006) *The Civil Sphere*. Oxford University Press, New York.

Alexander, J. C. (2003a) A Cultural Sociology of Evil. In J. C. Alexander, *The Meanings of Social Life: A Cultural Sociology*. Oxford University Press, New York, pp. 109–20.

Alexander, J. C. (2003b) Introduction: The Meanings of (Social) Life: On the Origins of a Cultural Sociology. In J. C. Alexander, *The Meanings of Social Life: A Cultural Sociology*. Oxford University Press, New York, pp. 3–10.

Alexander, J. C. (2001) Parsons as a Republican Critic of Industrial Society: A New Understanding of the Early Writings. In G. Pollini and G. Sciortino (eds.), *Parsons' The Structure of Social Action and Contemporary Debates*. Franco Angeli, Milan, pp. 15–24.

Alexander, J. C. (2000a) Theorizing the Good Society: Hermeneutic, Normative, and Empirical Discourses. *Canadian Journal of Sociology* 25(3), 271–309.

Alexander, J. C. (2000b) This Worldly Mysticism: Inner Peace and World Transformation in the Work and Life of Charles "Skip" Alexander. *Journal of Adult Development* 7(4), 267–72.

Alexander, J. C. (1998a) After Neofunctionalism: Action, Culture, and Civil Society. In J. C. Alexander, *Neofunctionalism and After*. Basil Blackwell, New York pp. 210–33.

Alexander, J. (1998b) Bush, Hussein, and the Cultural Preparation for War: Toward a More Symbolic Theory of Political Legitimation. *Epoche* 21(1), 1–14.

Alexander, J. C. (1998c) *Real Civil Societies: Dilemmas of Institutionalization*. Sage, London.

Alexander, J. C. (1995) *Fin-de-Siècle Social Theory: Relativism, Reduction, and the Problem of Reason*. Verso, London.

170

Alexander, J. C. (1992a) Citizen and Enemy as Symbolic Classification: On the Polarizing Discourse of Civil Society. In M. Fournier and M. Lamont (eds.), *Where Culture Talks: Exclusion and the Making of Society*. University of Chicago Press, Chicago, pp. 289–308.

Alexander, J. C. (1992b) The Fragility of Progress: An Interpretation of the Turn Toward Meaning in Eisenstadt's Later Work. *Acta Sociologica* 35, 85–94.

Alexander, J. C. (1992c) General Theory in the Postpositivist Mode: The Epistemological Dilemma and the Search for Present Reason. In S. Seidman and D. Wagner (eds.), *Postmodernism and Social Theory*. Basil Blackwell, New York, pp. 322–68.

Alexander, J. C. (1992d) Some Remarks on "Agency" in Recent Sociological Theory. *Perspectives* 15(1), 1–4.

Alexander, J. C. (1988a) Back to Lippman. *The New Republic* 198(5), 15–16.

Alexander, J. C. (1988b) Core Solidarity, Ethnic Outgroup, and Social Differentiation. In J. C. Alexander, *Action and Its Environments*. Columbia University Press, New York, pp. 78–106.

Alexander, J. C. (1988c) Durkheim's Problem and Differentiation Theory Today. In J. C. Alexander, *Action and Its Environments*. University of California Press, Berkeley.

Alexander, J. C. (1988d) *Durkheimian Sociology: Cultural Studies*. Cambridge University Press, Cambridge.

Alexander, J. C. (1987) Culture and Political Crisis: Watergate and Durkheimian Sociology. In J. C. Alexander (ed.) *Durkheimian Sociology: Cultural Studies*. Cambridge University Press, New York, pp. 187–224.

Alexander, J. C. (1985) Habermas's New Critical Theory: Problems and Prospects. *American Journal of Sociology* 91, 400–25.

Alexander, J. C. (1983a) *The Classical Attempt at Theoretical Synthesis: Max Weber, Vol. 3 of Theoretical Logic in Sociology*. University of California Press, Berkeley.

Alexander, J. C. (1983b) *The Modern Reconstruction of Classical Thought: Talcott Parsons, Vol. 4 of Theoretical Logic in Sociology*. University of California Press, Berkeley.

Alexander, J. C. and Jacobs, R. N. (1998) Mass Communication, Ritual, and Civil Society. In T. Liebes and J. Curran (eds.), *Media, Ritual, and Identity*. Routledge, London, pp. 23–41.

Alexander, J. C. and Loader, C. (1985) Max Weber on Churches and Sects in North America: An Alternative Path toward Rationalization. *Sociological Theory* 3(1), 1–13.

Alexander, J. C. and Pia Lara, M. (1996) Honneth's New Critical Theory of Recognition. *New Left Review* 220, 126–52.

Alexander, J. C. and Smith, P. (2005) The New Durkheim: An Introduction. In J. C. Alexander and P. Smith (eds.), *The Cambridge Companion to Durkheim*. Cambridge University Press, Cambridge, pp. 1–40.

Alexander, J. C. and Smith, P. (2003) The Discourse of American Civil Society. In J. C. Alexander, *The Meanings of Social Life: A Cultural Sociology*. Oxford University Press, New York, pp. 121–54.

Alexander, J. C. and Smith, P. (1993) The Discourse of American Civil Society: A New Proposal for Cultural Studies. *Theory and Society* 22(2), 151–207.

BIBLIOGRAPHY

Anderson, E. (1990) *Streetwise: Race, Class and Change in an Urban Community*. University of Chicago Press, Chicago.

Arendt, H. (1951) *The Origins of Totalitarianism*. Harcourt Brace Jovanovich, New York.

Aristotle (1962) *The Politics* (trans. E. Barker). Oxford University Press, London.

Arnett, J. J. (2004) *Emerging Adulthood: The Winding Road from the Late Teens through the Twenties*. Oxford University Press, New York.

Aron, R. (1975) *History and the Dialectic of Violence: An Analysis of Sartre's "Critique de la Rasion Dialectique."* Harper & Row, New York.

Aron, R. (1957) *The Opium of the Intellectuals*. W. W. Norton & Co, New York.

Baert, P. (2011) The Sudden Rise of French Existentialism: A Case-Study in the Sociology of Intellectual Life. *Theory and Society* 40(5), 619–44.

Barber, B. (1983) *The Logic and Limits of Trust*. Rutgers University Press, New Brunswick, NJ.

Bataille, G. (1986 [1957]) *Eroticism: Death and Sensuality*. City Light Books, San Francisco.

Bataille, G. (1985 [1957]) *Literature and Evil*. Marion Boyars, London.

Bauman, Z. (2001) Making and Unmaking of Strangers. In P. Beilharz (ed.), *The Bauman Reader*. Blackwell, Oxford, pp. 200–17.

Bauman, Z. (1989) *Modernity and the Holocaust*. Cornell University Press, Ithaca, NY.

Becker, C. (1932) *The Heavenly City of the Eighteenth-Century Philosophers*. Yale University Press, New Haven, CT.

Bell, D. (1976) *The Cultural Contradictions of Capitalism*. Heinemann, London.

Bellah, R. (2011) *Religion in Human Evolution: From the Paleolithic to the Axial Age*. Harvard University Press, Cambridge, MA.

Bellah, R. (1991) Religious Evolution. In R. Bellah, *Beyond Belief: Essays on Religion in a Post-Traditional World*. Harper & Row, New York, pp. 20–45.

Bellah, R. N. (1975) *The Broken Covenant: American Civil Religion in Time of Trial*. Seabury, New York.

Bellah, R. N., Madsen, R., Sullivan, W. M., Swidler, A. and Tipton, S. M. (1985) *Habits of the Heart: Individualism and Commitment in American Life*. University of California Press, Berkeley.

Benjamin, W. (1968 [1936]) The Work of Art in the Age of Mechanical Reproduction. In W. Benjamin, *Illuminations*. Schocken Books, New York, pp. 217–52.

Bernstein, R. J. (2001) Radical Evil: Kant at War with Himself. In M. Pia Lara (ed.), *Rethinking Evil*. University of California Press, Berkeley, pp. 55–85.

Best, J. (2004) *Deviance: Career of a Concept*. Wadsworth, Belmont, CA.

Bloch, R. (1985) *Visionary Republic: Millennial Themes in American Thought, 1756–1800*. Cambridge University Press, New York.

Braunthal, J. (1945) *In Search of the Millennium*. Gollancz, London.

Brubaker, R. (2002) *Citizenship and Nationhood in France and Germany*. Harvard University Press, Cambridge, MA.

Caillois, R. (1959) *Man and the Sacred*. Free Press, Glencoe, IL.

Campbell, C. (2007) *The Easternization of the West: A Thematic Account of Cultural Change in the Modern Era*. Paradigm, Boulder, CO.

172

Campbell, C. (1987) *The Romantic Ethic and the Spirit of Modern Consumerism*. Blackwell, London.

Cherry, C. (1970) *God's New Israel*. Prentice-Hall, Englewood Cliffs, NJ.

Cohen, J. and Arato, A. (1995) *Civil Society and Political Theory*. MIT Press, Cambridge, MA.

Cohen, S. (1972) *Folk Devils and Moral Panics: the Creation of the Mods and Rockers*. MacGibbon and Kee, London.

Coser, L. (1993) A Sociologist's Atypical Life. *Annual Review of Sociology* 19, 1–15.

Coser, L. (1965) The Stranger in the Academy. In L. Coser (ed.), *Georg Simmel*. Prentice-Hall, Englewood Cliffs, NJ.

Coser, L. (1958) Georg Simmel's Style of Work: A Contribution to the Sociology of the Sociologist. *American Journal of Sociology* 63, 635–41.

Cushman, T. (1998) The Reflexivity of Evil. Paper presented at the colloquium *The Questions of Evil*. University of Virginia, April 9.

Dahrendorf, R. (1959) *Class and Class Conflict in Industrial Society*. Stanford University Press, Stanford, CA.

Dewey J. (1966 [1916]) *Democracy and Education*. Free Press, New York.

Douglas, M. and Wildavsky, A. (1982) *Risk and Culture: An Essay on the Selection of Technical and Environmental Dangers*. University of California Press, Berkeley.

Duhamel, G. (1931) *America: The Menace Scenes: From the Life of the Future*, trans. C. M. Thompson. Houghton Mifflin, Boston, MA.

Durkheim, E. (1984 [1893]) *The Division of Labor in Society*. Free Press, New York.

Durkheim, E. (1965 [1911]) *The Elementary Forms of Religious Life*. Free Press, New York.

Dworkin, R. (1977) *Taking Rights Seriously*. Harvard University Press, Cambridge, MA.

Eco, U. (1986) The Return of the Middle Ages. In U. Eco, *Travels in Hyperreality*. Harcourt, New York, pp. 59–85.

Edles, L. (1998) *Symbol and Ritual in the New Spain*. Cambridge University Press, Cambridge.

Eisenstadt, S. N. (2003) *Comparative Civilizations and Multiple Modernities*. Brill Academic, New York.

Eisenstadt, S. N. (1999) *Fundamentalism, Sectarianism, and Revolution: The Jacobin Dimension of Modernity*. Cambridge University Press, Cambridge.

Eisenstadt, S. N. (1987) *European Civilization in a Comparative Perspective*. Norwegian University Press, Oslo.

Eisenstadt, S. N. (1982) The Axial Age: The Emergence of Transcendental Visions and the Rise of Clerics. *European Journal of Sociology* 23, 294–314.

Eisenstadt, S. N. (1978) *Revolution and the Transformation of Societies: A Comparative Study in Civilizations*. Free Press, New York.

Eisenstadt, S. N. (1968a) Charisma and Institution-Building: Max Weber and Modern Sociology. In S. N. Eisenstadt, *Power, Trust, and Meaning: Essays in Sociological Theory and Analysis*. University of Chicago Press, Chicago, pp. 167–201.

Eisenstadt, S. N. (1968b) Introduction. In S. N. Eisenstadt (ed.), *The Protestant Ethic and Modernization: A Comparative View.* Basic Books, New York, pp. 3–45.

Entrikin, N. (1991) *The Betweenness of Place.* Johns Hopkins University Press, Baltimore, MD.

Erikson, E. (1950) *Childhood and Society.* Norton, New York.

Erikson, K. (1966) *Wayward Puritans.* Wiley, New York.

Eyerman, R. and Jamison, A. (1991) *Social Movements: A Cognitive Approach.* Polity, London.

Falasca-Zamponi, S. (2011) *Rethinking the Political: The Sacred, Aesthetic Politics, and the College de Sociologie.* McGill-Queens University Press, Montreal.

Fanon, F. (1965) *The Wretched of the Earth.* MacGibbon & Kee, London.

Fass, P. (1979) *The Damned and the Beautiful: American Youth in the 1920s.* Oxford University Press, New York.

Ferrara, A. (2001) The Evil That Men Do: A Meditation on Radical Evil from a Postmetaphysical Point of View. In M. Pia Lara (ed.), *Rethinking Evil: Contemporary Perspectives.* University of California Press, Berkeley, pp. 172–88.

Foucault, M. (1993) About the Beginning of the Hermeneutics of the Self. *Political Theory* 21(2), 198–227.

Foucault, M. (1980) *The History of Sexuality, Vol. I: An Introduction.* Vintage, New York.

Foucault, M. (1975), *Discipline and Punish: The Birth of the Prison.* Allen Lane, London.

Freud, A. (1993 [1936]) *The Ego and the Mechanisms of Defense.* Karnac Books, London.

Freud, S. (1963 [1915]) Reflections upon War and Death. In S. Freud, *Character and Culture.* Collier, New York, pp. 107–33.

Freud, S. (1961 [1930]). *Civilization and Its Discontents.* Norton, New York.

Fromm, E. (1941) *Escape from Freedom.* Holt, Rinehart, & Winston, New York.

Frye, N. (1957) *The Anatomy of Criticism.* Princeton University Press, Princeton, NJ.

Furet, F. (1999) *The Passing of an Illusion: The Idea of Communism in the Twentieth Century.* University of Chicago Press, Chicago.

Fussell, P. (1975) *The Great War and Modern Memory.* Oxford University Press, Oxford.

Geertz, C. (1983) Common Sense as a Cultural System. In C. Geertz, *Local Knowledge.* Basic Books, New York, pp. 73–93.

Gerhadt, U. (2001) Parsons' Analysis of the Societal Community. In A. Javier Trevino (ed.), *Talcott Parsons Today.* Rowman & Littlefield, New York, pp. 177–222.

Gibson, J. W. (2009) *A Reenchanted World: The Quest for a New Kinship with Nature.* Henry Holt, New York.

Gibson, J. W. (1994) *Warrior Dreams: Paramilitary Culture in Post-Vietnam America.* Hill & Wang, New York.

Gibson, J. W. (1986) *The Perfect War.* Atlantic, New York.

Giddens, A. (1984) *The Constitution of Society.* Polity Press, London.

Giesen, B. (2011) Inbetweenness and Ambivalence. In J. C. Alexander, R. Jacobs, and P. Smith (eds.), *The Oxford Handbook of Cultural Sociology*. Oxford University Press, Oxford, pp. 788–804.

Giesen, B. (2004) The Trauma of Perpetrators: The Holocaust as the Traumatic Reference of German National Identity. In J. C. Alexander, R. Eyerman, B. Giesen, N. Smelser and P. Sztompka (eds.), *Cultural Trauma and Collective Identity*. University of California Press, Berkeley, pp. 112–54.

Giesen, B. (1998) *Intellectuals and the Nation*. Cambridge University Press, Cambridge.

Gill, C. B. (ed.) (1995) *Bataille: Writing the Sacred*. Routledge, New York.

Goffman, E. (1963) *Stigma: Notes on the Management of Spoiled Identity*. Prentice-Hall, Englewood Cliffs, NJ.

Goldhagen, D. J. (1996) *Hitler's Willing Executioners, Ordinary Germans and the Holocaust*. Alfred A. Knopf, New York.

Goodman, T. (2010) *Staging Solidarity: Truth and Reconciliation in the New South Africa*. Paradigm, Boulder, CO.

Goubert, P. (1988) *The Course of French History*. Routledge, London.

Habermas, J. (1984) *The Theory of Communicative Action, Vol. 1*. Heinemann, London.

Habermas, J. (1973) Labor and Interaction: Remarks on Hegel's Jena Philosophy of Mind. In *Theory and Practice* (trans. J. Viertel). Beacon Press, Boston, MA, pp. 142–69.

Harden, C. (1974) *Presidential Power and Accountability*. University of Chicago Press, Chicago.

Hart, N. (1985) *The Sociology of Health and Medicine*. Causeway Press, Lancashire, UK.

Hayman, R. (1987) *Sartre: A Life*. Simon & Schuster, New York.

Herf, J. (2006) *The Jewish Enemy: Nazi Propaganda during World War II and the Holocaust*. Harvard University Press, Cambridge, MA.

Herf, J. (1986) The "Holocaust" Reception in West Germany. In A. Rabinbach and J. Zipes (eds.), *Germans and Jews since the Holocaust: The Changing Situation in Western Germany*. Holmes and Meier, New York, pp. 208–33.

Higham, J. (1992) *Strangers in the Land: Patterns of American Nativism, 1860–1925*. Rutgers University Press, New Brunswick, NJ.

Holsinger, B. (2008) Empire, Apocalypse, and the 9/11 Premodern. *Critical Inquiry* 34, 468–90.

Holsinger, B. (2007) *Neomedievalism, Neoconservativism, and the War on Terror*, Prickly Paradigm Press, Chicago.

Honneth, A. (1995) *The Struggle for Recognition*. Verso, London.

Horkheimer, M. and Adorno, T. (1969) *Dialectic of Enlightenment*. Continuum Publishing, New York.

Hughes, H. S. (1975) *The Sea Change: The Migration of Social Thought, 1930–1965*. Harper & Row, New York.

Hughes, H. S. (1966) *The Obstructed Path: French Social Thought in the Years of Desperation, 1930–1960*. Harper & Row: New York.

Hughes, H. S. (1958) *Consciousness and Society: The Reconstruction of European Social Thought, 1890–1930*. Vintage, New York.

Hyams, E. (1973) *The Millennium Postponed*. Taplinger, New York.

Jacobs, R. (2000) *Race, Media and the Crisis of Civil Society: from Watts to Rodney King*. Cambridge University Press, New York.

Janik, A. and Toulmin, S. (1973) *Wittgenstein's Vienna*. Simon & Schuster, New York.

Johnson, P. (1983) *Modern Times: The World from the Twenties to the Eighties*. Harper & Row, New York.

Katz, J. (1988) *Seductions of Crime: Moral and Sensual Attractions in Doing Evil*. Basic Books, New York.

Keniston, K. (1965) *The Uncommitted: Alienated Youth in American Society*. Dell, New York.

Kopytoff, I. (1986) The Cultural Biography of Things: Commoditization as Process. In A. Appadurai (ed.), *The Social Life of Things: Commodities in Cultural Perspective*. Cambridge University Press, Cambridge, pp. 64–91.

Kraft, S. (1994) Crackdown by Color in France: The government is targeting dark-skinned people in a hunt for Islamic terrorists. But critics also link the sweeps to bias against an immigrant group that refuses to give up its culture. *Los Angeles Times*, September 28, A1.

Kuhn, T. (1962) *The Structure of Scientific Revolutions*. University of Chicago Press, Chicago.

Kuisel, R. (1993) *Seducing the French: The Dilemma of Americanization*. University of California Press, Berkeley.

Lamont, M. (2000) *The Dignity of Working Men: Morality and the Boundaries of Race, Class, and Immigration*. Russell Sage Foundation, New York.

Lamont, M. (1992) *Money, Manners, and Morals*. University of Chicago Press, Chicago.

Lang, R. D. (1966) *The Divided Self*. Penguin, London.

Lanham, R. (1976) *The Motives of Elegance: Literary Rhetoric in the Renaissance*. Yale University Press, New Haven, CT.

Le Corbusier (1986 [1931]) *Toward an Architecture*. Dover Publications, New York.

Lerner, M. (1987) Bork's progress. *The New Republic*, 197, 18–20.

Levine, D. N. (1981) Rationality and Freedom: Weber and Beyond. *Sociological Inquiry* 51, 5–25.

Levinson, D. (1978) *Seasons of a Man's Life*. Knopf, New York.

Lévi-Strauss, C. (1974 [1955]) *Tristes Tropiques*. Atheneum, London.

Lévi-Strauss, C. (1963) Structural Analysis in Linguistics and Anthropology. *Structural Anthropology* 1, 31–54.

Llobera, J. R. (1988) The Dark Side of Modernity. Paper presented at Madrid Conference on the History of Sociology, Madrid Spain, May.

Loewenstein, K. (1966) *Max Weber's Political Ideas in the Perspective of Our Time*. University of Massachusetts Press, Cambridge, MA.

Löwith, K. (1982) *Max Weber and Karl Marx*. Allen & Unwin, London.

Löwith, K. (1949) *Meaning in History*. University of Chicago Press, Chicago.

Luhmann, N. (1982) Durkheim on Morality and the "Division of Labor." In *The Differentiation of Society*, Columbia University Press, New York, pp. 3–20.

Lukács, G. (1971 [1924]) *History and Class Consciousness*. MIT Press, Cambridge, MA.

176

Lynch, G. (2012) *The Sacred in the Modern World*. Oxford University Press, Oxford.

Maccoby, H. (1992) *Judas Iscariot and the Myth of Jewish Evil*. Free Press, New York.

MacIntyre, A. (1981) *After Virtue*. Notre Dame University Press, South Bend, IN.

Magnuson, E. (1997) Ideological Conflict in American Political Culture. *International Journal of Sociology and Social Policy* 17(6), 84–130.

Mannheim, K. (1940) *Man and Society in an Age of Reconstruction: Studies in Modern Social Structure*. Routledge & Kegan Paul, London.

Marcuse, H. (1964) *One-Dimensional Man*. Beacon, Boston, MA.

Marshall, T. H. (1964) *Class, Citizenship, and Social Development*. Doubleday, Garden City, NY.

Massey, D. and Denton, N. (1993) *American Apartheid: Segregation and the Making of the Underclass*. Harvard University Press, Cambridge, MA.

Mast, J. (2012) *The Performative Presidency: Crisis and Resurrection During the Clinton Years*. Cambridge University Press, New York.

Mayhew, L. (1997) *The New Public*. Cambridge University Press, New York.

Mayhew, L. (1968) Ascription in Modern Society. *Sociological Inquiry* 38, 105–20.

Merton, R. K. (1970 [1939]) *Science, Technology, and Society in Seventeenth-Century England*. Harper & Row, New York.

Michels, R. (1961 [1911]) *Political Parties: A Sociological Study of the Oligarchical Tendencies of Modern Democracy*. Free Press, New York.

Miller, D. (1998) *A Theory of Shopping*. Polity, London.

Miller, J. (1993) *The Passion of Michel Foucault*. Simon and Schuster, New York.

Miller, P. (1967) *Nature's Nation*. Harvard University Press, Cambridge, MA.

Miller, P. (1965) *The Life of the Mind in America*. Harcourt Brace, New York.

Miller, P. (1956) *Errand into the Wilderness*. Harvard University Press, Cambridge, MA.

Mitzman, A. (1970) *The Iron Cage: An Historical Interpretation of Max Weber*. Knopf, New York.

Mommsen, W. J. (1974) *The Age of Bureaucracy*. Oxford University Press, Oxford.

Morgan, E. S. (1958) *The Puritan Dilemma*. Little, Brown, and Company, Boston, MA.

Mosse, G. L. (1964) *The Crisis of German Ideology: Intellectual Origins of the Third Reich*. Grosset & Dunlap, New York.

Nietzsche, F. (1956 [1872, 1887]) *The Birth of Tragedy and the Genealogy of Morals*. Doubleday, New York.

Nolte, E. (1966) *Three Faces of Fascism*. Holt, Rinehart & Winston, New York.

Oakeshott, M. (1962) *Rationalism in Politics and other Essays*. Methuen, New York.

O'Hara, M. (2005) Walking the Happy Talk. *The Guardian*, Society Section, November 30.

Ovid (2004) *Metamorphoses* (trans. D. Raeburn). Penguin, New York, I: pp. 7–9, 32–3, 88.

Parkin, F. (1979) *Marxism and Class Theory: A Bourgeois Critique*. Tavistock, London.

Parks, M. (1988) History Tests Cancelled for Soviet Youngsters: Decision, Affecting 53 Million, Will Provide Time to Correct Stalinist "Lies," Izvestia Says. *Los Angeles Times*. Retrieved July 27, 2012 from http://articles.latimes.com/1988-06-11/news/mn-4263_1_soviet-history.

Parsons, T. (1977) Law as an Intellectual Stepchild. *Sociological Inquiry* 47(3–4), 11–57.

Parsons, T. (1973) *The System of Modern Societies*. Prentice-Hall, Englewood Cliffs, NJ.

Parsons, T. (1969a) On the Concept of Influence. In T. Parsons, *Politics and Social Structures*. Free Press, New York, pp. 405–38.

Parsons, T. (1969b) On the Concept of Value Commitments. In T. Parsons, *Politics and Social Structures*. Free Press, New York, pp. 439–72.

Parsons, T. (1968) On the Concept of Value-Commitments. *Sociological Inquiry* 38, 135–60.

Parsons, T. (1967) Some Reflections on the Place of Force in Social Process. In T. Parsons, *Sociological Theory and Modern Society*. Free Press, New York, pp. 264–96.

Parsons, T. (1966a) *Societies: Evolutionary and Comparative Perspectives*. Prentice-Hall, Englewood Cliffs, NJ.

Parsons, T. (1966b) Full Citizenship for the Negro American? In K. Clark and T. Parsons (eds.), *The Negro American*. Houghton Mifflin, Boston, MA.

Parsons, T. (1954) *Essays in Sociological Theory*. Free Press, New York.

Parsons, T. (1951) *The Social System*. Free Press, New York.

Parsons, T. (1937) *The Structure of Social Action*. Free Press, New York.

Parsons, T. and Shils, E. (eds.) (1951) Values, Motives, and Systems of Action. In *Towards a General Theory of Action*. Harvard University Press, Cambridge, MA.

Parsons, T. and Smelser, N. (1956) *Economy and Society*. Free Press, New York.

Pevsner, N. (1977) *Pioneers of Modern Design from William Morris to Walter Gropius*. Penguin, Harmondsworth.

Pía Lara, M. (ed.) (2001) *Rethinking Evil*. University of California Press, Berkeley.

Piaget, J. (1972) *Principles of Genetic Epistemology*. Routledge & Kegan Paul, London.

Plato (1965) *The Republic* (trans. F. M. Comford). Oxford University Press, New York.

Polanyi, K. (1957) *The Great Transformation*. Beacon, Boston, MA.

Poster, M. (1979) *Sartre's Marxism*. Pluto Press, London.

Propp, V. (1969 [1928]) *Morphology of the Folk-tale*. University of Texas Press, Austin.

Rawls, J. (1971) *A Theory of Justice*. Harvard University Press, Cambridge, MA.

Reed, I. A. (2007) Why Salem Made Sense: Culture, Gender, and the Puritan Persecution of Witchcraft. *Cultural Sociology* 1, 209–34.

Reed, I. A. (2011) *Interpretation and Social Knowledge: On the Use of Theory in the Human Sciences*. University of Chicago Press, Chicago, IL.

Rhodes, R. (1988) *The Making of the Atomic Bomb*. Simon & Schuster, New York.

Richardson, M. (1994) *Georges Bataille*. Routledge, New York.

Richman, M. (1995) The Sacred Group: A Durkheimian Perspective on the Collège de Sociologie. In C. B. Gill (ed.), *Bataille: Writing the Sacred*. Routledge, London, pp. 58–76.

Rieff, P. (1968) *The Triumph of the Therapeutic: Uses of Faith after Freud*. Harper & Row, New York.

Riesman, D. (1950) *The Lonely Crowd*. Yale University Press, New Haven, CT.

Ringer, F. K. (1969) *The Decline of the German Mandarins: The German Academic Community, 1890–1933*. Harvard University Press, Cambridge, MA.

Roberge, J. (2012) The Aesthetic Public's Sphere and the Transformation of Criticism. *Social Semiotics* 21(3), 435–53.

Roberge, J. (2011) Critics as Cultural Intermediaries. In C. Fleck and A. Hess (eds.), *Public Knowledge for Whom?* Ashgate, London.

Rorty, R. (1979) *Philosophy and the Mirror of Nature*. Princeton University Press, Princeton, NJ.

Roszack, T. (1969) *The Making of a Counter-Culture: Reflections on the Technocratic Society and Its Youthful Opposition*. Doubleday, Garden City, NY.

Sahlins, M. (1976) Le Pensée Bourgeoise. In M. Sahlins, *Culture and Practical Reason*. University of Chicago Press, Chicago, pp. 166–204.

Said, E. (1978) *Orientalism*. Random House, New York.

Sartre, J. P. (1976 [1968]) *Critique of Dialectical Reason*. New Left Books, London.

Sartre, J. P. (1956 [1943]) *Being and Nothingness*. Washington Square Press, New York.

Saussure, F. de (1959 [1911]) *Course in General Linguistics*. McGraw-Hill, New York.

Schaefer, D. (1965 [1908]) A Contemporary Academic View of Georg Simmel. In L. Coser (ed.), *Georg Simmel*. Prentice-Hall, Englewood Cliffs, NJ, pp. 37–9.

Schluchter, W. (1984) The Paradox of Rationalization: On the Relation of Ethics to the World. In G. Roth and W. Schluchter (eds.), *Max Weber's Vision of History*. University of California Press, Berkeley, pp. 11–64.

Schluchter, W. (1981) *The Rise of Western Rationalism: Max Weber's Developmental History*. University of California Press, Berkeley.

Schmidt, I. (2014) Perpetual Trauma and Its Organizations: MADD and Drunk-Driving Revisited. *Memory Studies* 7(2).

Schudson, M. (2008) *Why Democracies Need an Unlovable Press*. Polity, London.

Sciortino, G. (2001) How Different Can We Be? Parsons' Societal Community, Pluralism: The Multicultural Debate. In R. Fox, V. Lidz, and H. Bershady (eds.), *After Parsons: A Theory of Social Action for the Twenty-First Century*. Russell Sage Foundation, New York, pp. 111–36.

Seidman, S. (2013) Defilement and Disgust: Theorizing the Other. *American Journal of Cultural Sociology* 1(1), forthcoming.

Seidman, S. (2003) *The Social Construction of Sexuality*. Norton, New York.

Seidman, S. (1983a) *Liberalism and the Origins of European Social Theory*. University of California Press, Berkeley.

Seidman, S. (1983b) Modernity, Meaning and Cultural Pessimism in Max Weber. *Sociological Analysis* 44, 267–78.

Sheehy, G. (1974) *Passages: Predictable Passages of Adult Life*. Random House, New York.

Shils, E. (1975) Charisma, Order and Status. In E. Shils (ed.), *Center and Periphery: Essays in Macro-Sociology*. University of Chicago Press, Chicago.

Simmel, G. (1950) The Stranger. In K. Wolff (ed.), *The Sociology of Georg Simmel*. Free Press of Glencoe, New York, pp. 402–8.

Skinner, Q. (1978) *The Foundations of Modern Political Thought*. Cambridge University Press, Cambridge.

Slater, P. (1970) *The Pursuit of Loneliness: American Culture at the Breaking Point*. Beacon, Boston, MA.

Slotkin, R. (1973) *Regeneration through Violence: The Mythology of the American Frontier, 1600–1860*. Wesleyan University Press, Middletown, CT.

Smith, P. (2008) *Punishment and Culture*. University of Chicago Press, Chicago.

Smith, P. (2005) *Why War?: The Cultural Logic of Iraq, the Gulf War, and Suez*. University of Chicago Press, Chicago.

Smith, P. (1998) Barbarism and Civility in the Discourses of Fascism, Communism, and Democracy. In J. C. Alexander (ed.), *Real Civil Societies*. Sage, London, pp. 115–37.

Smith, P. (1991) Codes and Conflict: Toward a Theory of War as Ritual. *Theory and Society* 20, 103–38.

Sorel, G. (1950 [1908]) *Reflections on Violence*. Collier, New York.

Steiner, F. (1956) *Taboo*. Cohen and West, London.

Steinmetz, G. (2007) *The Devil's Handwriting: Precoloniality and the German Colonial State in Qingdoa, Samoa and Southwest Africa*. University of Chicago Press, Chicago.

Stivers, R. (1982) *Evil in Modern Myth and Ritual*. University of Georgia Press, Atlanta.

Taylor, C. (1989) *Sources of the Self: The Making of Modern Identity*. Harvard University Press, Cambridge, MA.

Taylor, C. (1975) *Hegel*. Cambridge University Press, Cambridge.

Tenbruck, F. (1974) Max Weber and the Sociology of Science: A Case Reopened. *Zeitschrift für Soziologie* 3(6), 312–20.

Thompson, K. (1998) *Moral Panics*. Routledge, London.

Tillich, P. (1952) *The Courage to Be*. Yale University Press, New Haven, CT.

Tiryakian, E. (1975) Neither Marx nor Durkheim . . . Perhaps Weber. *American Journal of Sociology* 81(1), 1–33.

Touraine, A. (1992) Social Movements, Revolution and Democracy. In R. Schurmann (ed.), *The Public Realm*. State University of New York Press, Buffalo, pp. 268–83.

Turner, V. (1969). *The Ritual Process*. Aldine, Chicago.

Tuveson, E. L. (1968) *Redeemer Nation*. University of Chicago Press, Chicago.

Wagner-Pacifici, R. (1986) *The Moro Morality Play: Terrorism as Social Drama*. University of Chicago Press, Chicago.

Walzer, M. (1983) *Spheres of Justice*. Basic Books, New York.

Walzer, M. (1965) *Revolution of the Saints*. Harvard University Press, Cambridge, MA.

Weber, M. (1985) Church and Sect in North America. *Sociological Theory* 3, 7–13.

Weber, M. (1978) *Economy and Society*. University of California Press, Berkeley.

Weber, M. (1958 [1904–5]) *The Protestant Ethic and the Spirit of Capitalism*. Scribner and Sons, New York.

Weber, M. (1946a [1917]) Politics as a Vocation. In H. Gerth and C. Wright Mills (eds.), *From Max Weber*. Oxford University Press, New York, pp. 77–128.

Weber, M. (1946b [1917]) Religious Rejections of the World and Their Directions. In H. Gerth and C. Wright Mills (eds.), *From Max Weber*. Oxford University Press, New York, pp. 323–59.

Weber, M. (1946c [1917]) Science as a Vocation. In H. Gerth and C. Wright Mills (eds.), *From Max Weber*. Oxford University Press, New York, pp. 129–56.

Williams, R. M. (1971) Change and Stability in Values and Value Systems. In B. Barber and A. Inkeles (eds.), *Stability and Social Change*. Little, Brown, Boston, MA, pp. 123–59.

Wilson, W. J. (1987) *The Truly Disadvantaged: The Inner City, the Underclass, and Public Policy*. University of Chicago Press, Chicago.

Wittgenstein, L. (1980) *Culture and Value*. University of Chicago Press, Chicago.

Wittgenstein, L. (1968 [1945]) *Philosophical Investigations*. Macmillan, New York.

Wittgenstein, L. (1922) *Tractatus Logico-Philosophicus*. Harcourt, Brace, New York.

Yeo, E. (1981) Christianity in Chartist Struggle, 1838–1842. *Past and Present* 91, 109–39.

INDEX